P9-AQJ-251

The Performing Arts

The Other Rockefeller Panel Reports, Contained in One Volume Entitled Prospect for America:

The Mid-Century Challenge to U.S. Foreign Policy
International Security: The Military Aspect
Foreign Economic Policy for the Twentieth Century
The Challenge to America: Its Economic and Social Aspects
The Pursuit of Excellence: Education and the Future of America
The Power of the Democratic Idea

THE PERFORMING ARTS

Rockefeller Panel Report on the future of theatre, dance, music in America

PROBLEMS AND PROSPECTS

McGraw-Hill Book Company
New York
Toronto
London
Sydney

The Performing Arts:
Problems and Prospects

Library of Congress
Catalog Number: 65–16153
FIRST EDITION

Foreword by the Chairman

This report on the state of the performing arts in the United States is intended as a challenge, not an answer.

Its purpose is to present a thoughtful assessment of the place of the performing arts in our national life and to identify the impediments to their greater welfare and to their wider enjoyment. Because the aim of this report is to suggest, to guide, to help point the way, its conclusions can be neither definitive nor final.

Only in our time have we begun to recognize the arts as a community concern to be placed alongside our long-accepted responsibilities for libraries, museums, hospitals, and schools. In the two decades since World War II, our society has achieved material advances almost beyond belief. Yet man increasingly realizes that meeting basic physical needs falls far short of attaining the end objectives of life—the emotional, intellectual, and aesthetic satisfactions that constitute his higher needs. The arts today are more fully appreciated as one means by which man can achieve the satisfactions he seeks, and therefore are important, even essential, to the human mind and spirit.

If the arts are vital to a mature civilization, how do they best flourish? What organizations are needed to nour-

ish them? How are they to be supported and maintained? Questions such as these, especially when applied to the performing arts, need public discussion and are worthy of thoughtful inquiry and debate. For these reasons, in the fall of 1963, *the Rockefeller Brothers Fund asked a group of citizens from all parts of the country who are identified with many segments of American life to join in a study of the future development and support of the performing arts in the United States.*

From the beginning, the panel had particularly in mind a study that would be useful to those responsible for the direction and management of performing arts institutions. We also wanted to be helpful to foundation and corporate executives who are considering support for the arts. We hoped, too, that the study might be of value to local, state, and federal officials as the arts become increasingly important to the well-being and happiness of the people. And finally, we wished to serve private citizens who are working to enhance the quality of life in their communities.

For their dedication to the purposes of the study, I would like to express my personal appreciation to all members of the panel. Many absented themselves from their businesses or other interests to devote long hours to the work. They gave generously of their time and their thoughts. That national leaders such as these are concerned to this extent with the state of the performing arts in America augurs well for the future.

John D. Rockefeller 3rd

Contents

Preface by the Panel

In this report, we hope to engage the attention of the American people and to waken their concern about the performing arts in the United States. For in spite of tremendous growth and exciting promise, the performing arts as we see them today are in trouble. If we succeed in illuminating some of the problems facing the arts, stimulating public discussion, and stirring action by those concerned, we believe this study will be a valuable successor to the six earlier Rockefeller Panel Reports. These, issued between 1958 and 1961, had acknowledged impact on national thought and focused fresh attention on the opportunities confronting American democracy in foreign policy, in military preparedness, in education, and in social and economic affairs.

In compiling background for our discussions, the panel found the organizations and institutions of the arts extremely cooperative. Nevertheless, we encountered considerable difficulty in obtaining adequate information. Our experience confirms our judgment that among the key problems of the performing arts in America today are the lack of sufficient data and a central source of information.

In the course of this project, we have deliberated for

more than eighty hours at five two-day meetings. We have heard forty witnesses expert in the arts as well as in government, in education, in management, in labor. Our discussions have been supplemented by the work of special subcommittees on particular aspects of the project. We have reviewed some thirty authoritative papers detailing the problems confronting music, opera, dance, and theatre. In addition, over four hundred persons were interviewed by the staff individually or in small groups.

One hundred corporations were surveyed by questionnaire to determine corporate attitudes. Seventy-five officials of philanthropic institutions and performing arts organizations presented their thoughts and observations on foundation programs. Eight states and forty-seven municipalities were surveyed as to their degree of activity in support of the arts. A complementary study, concentrating on a detailed economic analysis of the performing arts, has been conducted simultaneously by the Twentieth Century Fund. The two studies have been closely coordinated, and a continuing exchange of information has been achieved.

We would like to express our gratitude to the Special Studies section of the Rockefeller Brothers Fund. Under the direction of Nancy Hanks the staff has worked effectively with diligence and enthusiasm. One of our panel members, Dexter Keezer, has served us expertly in giving our report form based on our discussions. We were ably assisted also by Norris Houghton and in the final stages of writing by Richard Schickel.

This is the first time that a comprehensive report on the state of the performing arts has been attempted. Although not every member of the panel subscribes to every detail, the report reflects our substantial agreement. It is breaking new ground and providing factual material that has not previously been assembled. Agreement with our findings would be gratifying, but continuing consideration that leads to effective results would be more rewarding.

Patricia M. Baillargeon, former assistant to Mrs. Eleanor Roosevelt; board member, Seattle Repertory Theatre and Seattle Youth Symphony; Seattle.

Walker L. Cisler, chairman of the board, Detroit Edison Company; director, Detroit Symphony Orchestra; Detroit.

Kenneth N. Dayton, vice president, Dayton's; director and past president, Minnesota Orchestral Association; Minneapolis.

T. Keith Glennan, president, Case Institute of Technology; Cleveland.

Samuel B. Gould, president, State University of New York; former president, Educational Broadcasting Corporation; Albany.

William B. Hartsfield, mayor emeritus of Atlanta; trustee, Atlanta Symphony Orchestra and Atlanta Music Festival Association; Atlanta.

August Heckscher, director, Twentieth Century Fund; former special consultant on the arts to President Kennedy; trustee, National Repertory Theatre Foundation; New York.

Margaret Hickey, senior editor, public affairs, *Ladies' Home Journal;* St. Louis.

Norris Houghton, chairman, Department of Drama, Vassar College; co-founder, Phoenix Theatre; New York.

Devereux C. Josephs, former chairman of the board, New York Life Insurance Company; vice chairman of the board, Lincoln Center for the Performing Arts; trustee, Metropolitan Museum of Art and New York Public Library; New York.

Abbott Kaplan, director, University of California Extension, Los Angeles; chairman of the board, Theatre Group; chairman, California Arts Commission; Los Angeles.

Dexter M. Keezer, economic advisor, McGraw-Hill, Inc.; New York.

Louis Kronenberger, professor of theatre arts, Brandeis University; member, National Institute of Arts and Letters; Waltham, Massachusetts.

Warner Lawson, dean, College of Fine Arts, Howard University; conductor, Howard University choirs; member, advisory committee on the arts, State Department, and advisory committee, John F. Kennedy Center for the Performing Arts; Washington, D.C.

John H. MacFadyen, architect, MacFadyen and Knowles; former executive director, New York State Council on the Arts; New York.

Stanley Marcus, president, Neiman-Marcus; director, Community Arts Fund of Dallas, Dallas Symphony Orchestra, and Dallas Theatre Center; Dallas.

Henry Allen Moe, president and chairman of the board, New York State Historical Association; president, American Philosophical Society; New York.

James F. Oates, Jr., chairman of the board and chief executive officer, Equitable Life Assurance Society; trustee, American Museum of Natural History; New York.

Perry T. Rathbone, director, Boston Museum of Fine Arts; trustee, New England Conservatory of Music and Boston Arts Festival; Boston.

Oliver Rea, managing director, Minnesota Theatre Company Foundation, Tyrone Guthrie Theatre; president, Theatre Communications Group, Inc.; Minneapolis.

Joseph Verner Reed, Sr., chairman of the board and executive producer, American Shakespeare Festival Theatre and Academy (Stratford, Connecticut); New York.

John D. Rockefeller 3rd, chairman of the panel; chairman of the board, Lincoln Center for the Performing Arts and Rockefeller Foundation; New York.

Samuel R. Rosenbaum, trustee, Recording Industries Music Performance Trust Funds; member, board of directors, Philadelphia Orchestra Association; Philadelphia.

Emile H. Serposs, director, Division of Music, Chicago Public Schools; member, board of directors, Music Educators National Conference; Chicago.

Charles M. Spofford, partner, Davis Polk Wardwell Sunderland and Kiendl; director and chairman, executive committee, Metropolitan Opera Association; vice chairman of the board and chairman of the executive committee, Lincoln Center for the Performing Arts; New York.

Frank Stanton, president, Columbia Broadcasting System; member, board of directors, Lincoln Center for the Performing Arts, New York.

James A. Suffridge, international president, Retail Clerks International Association; Washington, D.C.

Helen M. Thompson, executive vice president, American Symphony Orchestra League; member, National Music Council and National Council on the Arts and Government; Vienna, Virginia.

Frazar B. Wilde, chairman of the board, Connecticut General Life Insurance Company; Hartford.

Harold Lionel Zellerbach, chairman, executive committee, Crown Zellerbach Corporation; president, San Francisco Art Commission; director, San Francisco Ballet Guild; trustee, California Legion of Honor Art Museum; San Francisco.

SPECIAL STUDIES PROJECT STAFF

Nancy Hanks

George Alan Smith **Alan L. Campbell**

Julie North Chelminski, Janet English Gracey, Nancy Lassiter Huggin, Marian Q. Jackson, Charles S. King, Jr., Nancy D. LaBarbera, Sylvia Drucker Mavis, Elizabeth Moss Schmidt

1
The Arts in America

Observers of American society, since the establishment of the Republic, have proclaimed the incompatibility of democracy with the attainment of high standards of excellence in the arts. A significant minority, however, has never accepted this judgment. This minority has sought to prove two things: that democracy is as capable of fostering works of artistic excellence as any aristocracy and, more important, that it is capable of creating a far broader audience for them than any other form of society. Indeed, there have long been thoughtful people among us who believe that the ultimate test of democracy lies in the quality of the artistic and intellectual life it creates and supports.

It has, however, taken a long time for this view to receive wide currency. "In the eighteenth century," as Eric Larrabee has noted, "the question that preoccupied thoughtful people in the United States was the achieving of political democracy—and in the main we answered it. In the nineteenth century, the question was one of achieving economic democracy—and we answered that, too, at least in theory and potentiality. In the twentieth century, the main challenge to the United States is the achieving of cultural democracy—but that still remains very far indeed from being answered."

This is true. But what is significant is that the question of achieving cultural democracy—and the ways and means of doing it—has become a question that many are asking and many are actively working to answer.

In 1876, Henry James drew a portrait of *The American* for whom "the world . . . was a great bazaar, where one might stroll about and purchase handsome things"; and to whom "an undue solicitude for 'culture' seemed a sort of silly dawdling . . . a proceeding properly confined to women, foreigners, and other unpractical persons." There were virtues in the national stereotype James created. His American, the classic self-made man, was strong and independent, sure of himself and proud of his values. He was, in fact, a type ideally suited to succeed in his time and place—and to build the basic institutions that are today the bedrock of our national strength.

But this earlier American, with his taste for doing and building rather than contemplation, with his faith that progress could be achieved almost exclusively through commercial and technological means, is no longer the exclusive ideal in today's world. James was ironical about him, but by the 1920's an entire generation of novelists was satirizing this early American in more brutal fashion. By our own time many were ready to tax him with serious questions. How dare he view the world as "a great bazaar" to "stroll about" with such casual arrogance, buying culture instead of creating it in his native land? How could he regard culture as "a sort of silly dawdling"? Where was his sense of responsibility? His sense of mission? Didn't he understand the imperatives of the spirit and the mind? Didn't he understand that in history's final analysis a nation would be judged by the quality of the civilization it achieved, not by its material well-being?

Such questions, of course, betray a lack of reality about the nature of material well-being and the nature of art. Unless a civilization possesses the former in some measure, it will have neither the time nor the energy to cultivate the latter. But the truly important thing is that in our time we feel impelled to ask the questions. Within our reach is the possibility of developing a standard of living assuring education and leisure in undreamed-of abundance; our economy has transformed work, making it less physically taxing; at the same time it has raised the individual's level of productivity, freeing more of his time for pursuits often more stimulating than those of the working day; social and welfare programs have tempered the impact of age-old social and physical hazards.

The first result of these changing conditions has been an emphasis on material acquisition and passive enjoyment. It is true that many individual wants remain unsatisfied. It is also true that our productive system, with its marvelous capacity for innovation, will continue to open new fields for the consumer. But there is a growing realization that simple materialism cannot permanently satisfy a society, that political and economic progress alone cannot satisfy spiritual hunger, that entertainment which makes no demand upon the mind or the body offers neither a permanent enrichment of the spirit nor a full measure of delight.

With this realization has come a general re-evaluation of the role of the arts in society. We are beginning to see them as the culmination of other achievements—the attainment that in the end gives a society its hope for a lasting place in history and its people the chance for the fullest freedom and happiness.

When President John F. Kennedy dedicated a new library at Amherst College in 1963, he was, in effect, summarizing a developing consensus, not making a ritual obeisance to the arts, when he said: "I see little of more importance to the future of our country and our civilization than full recognition of the place of the artist. If art is to nourish the roots of our culture, society must set the artist free to follow his vision wherever it takes him. . . . art is not a form of propaganda, it is a form of truth. . . . art establishes the basic human truths which must serve as the touchstones of our judgment."

But setting the artist free is no easy matter. Our democratic political institutions guarantee his legal right to speak freely, and our tradition of concern for civil liberties insures him of defenders when that freedom is challenged—as it still too often is. But freedom for the artist involves a great deal more than this, for the speech of great art is neither casual nor hurried. More than most people, the artist needs time to measure his words and select his images if he is to speak in his truest voice. That he should have time is of the essence, and thus far we have not, generally speaking, been overly generous in helping our artists find it. Nor have we been particularly generous in providing the means by which completed works can be presented. Some artists, notably the composer and the choreographer and the playwright, require the existence of theatres or concert halls before their work can be seen or heard. Beyond that, all of these artists need highly skilled performers, who are creative in their own terms, to present their work most effectively. These performing artists require expensive and extensive training to bring their talents to that pitch where they can fully realize and communicate all the meaning and nuance of the primary creator's work. They also need time to prepare works for performance. They, too, require a reasonable measure of economic security in order to concentrate fully on the work at hand. And they, like all artists, require periods when they need not work at all—for simple relaxation, for contemplation, for study, for that recharging of the spirit without which they cannot bring their best to their professions.

Perhaps most important of all, both the creative artist and the performing artist need an intelligent and understanding audience. If an audience cannot appreciate the magnificent and continuing dialogue that makes the artist relate to the present as well as the past, then there is little hope that a work of art will arouse the sense of drama and conflict without which art ceases to be a living, vital matter and deteriorates to something merely "appreciated." When this occurs, art becomes the creature of empty fashion, blown by the artificial winds of publicity.

Effective development of the arts is, then, a complex matter. It becomes, in our time and country, a matter of creating new organizational arrangements—for teaching, for performing, for supporting the artist. It becomes a matter of developing an audience as much as it does of training the artist. It becomes a matter of money, of energy, of time. It is also, of course, an unprecedented challenge for democracy. For we are seeking to create cultural institutions that will serve huge numbers of people—more than any cultural establishment of any other time or place has tried to serve. We are seeking to demonstrate that there is no incompatibility between democracy and high artistic standards. And we are seeking to do so on a grand scale.

It is premature to regard the developing consensus about the importance of the arts as fully formed. There are influential voices among us who question the expenditure of so much of our treasure upon the arts, the values of which cannot be charted like the movements of the solar system, or demonstrated by a litmus test, or worked out mathematically to the *n*th decimal place. Others are convinced that political freedom coupled with the maintenance of the free enterprise system is enough for the artist, and enough for society to undertake, given its many other burdens. They require information on the practical, immediate, *social* benefits of the arts. It is very much in the American character to demand such proofs.

It is difficult for artists themselves to offer these proofs. They are firm in the conviction that art is its own reward, that it is inevitably degraded if it is justified in secondary or utilitarian terms. About as far as they care to go is to agree with President Kennedy that "art establishes the basic human truths which must serve as the touchstones of our judgment." Some might press on a little further and note that while the arts do not make society or its individual members more energetic or efficient, they do tend to make both wiser and happier—inwardly healthier, outwardly more alive. The arts are a source of simple enjoyment and delight, hence, of refreshment and renewal. They are also educating and civilizing, can provide a sense of the grace, power, enchantment, and beauty of which the creative impulse is capable. And, at their greatest, the arts are exalting, with some of religion's moral and mystical power.

These are the terms in which the arts are best justified. Yet there are others.

William James observed that the strength of any society is best judged by the creativeness it induces in its citizens. Crawford H. Greenewalt, chairman of the board of E. I. du Pont de Nemours and Company, has remarked that it is not so much in the volume as in the spread of its creative effort that this strength lies. A society characterized by a serious lack of interest in or attention to a classically important area of human endeavor does not fully serve the aspirations of all its people. Nor does it realize its full strength in the present or prepare adequately for the future. "The society which creates scientists by diminishing the ranks of its philosophers may in the end have little need for either." Thus, at a time when the United States is perforce heavily engaged at the expanding frontiers of science, at a moment when many of its best educated citizens are engaged in the massive scientific and technological effort that so characterizes our civilization, a thriving development of the arts is essential to a well and safely balanced society.

Increased leisure also creates a social imperative for the development of the arts. It has been clearly demonstrated that the use of this leisure can be both an individual and a community problem if it is not channeled into constructive and satisfying ranges of activity such as the arts afford. As stated by Thomas J. Watson, Jr., chairman of the board of International Business Machines Corporation: ". . . the greater our skills in the humanities—in literature and the arts—the greater our capacity for the constructive use of leisure time, which is bound to increase as machines lift old burdens from men's shoulders and minds."

For young people the arts offer a way of finding themselves in what they often view as a baffling world. They have even been effective in reaching those who are deeply troubled. For example, the Henry Street Settlement in New York City reports that it is finding "through the arts—through music, acting, the dance—a way of reaching delinquent, emotionally ill, and neglected children and helping them to raise their sights and take steps toward realizing socially useful lives."

When the arts go abroad, as they are in increasing degree through cultural exchanges, they can disclose the vital and creative aspects of the countries originating them. They can make a distinct, if not precisely measurable, contribution to increasing international understanding. Also, the overseas tours of our artists help to counter the widespread view that the United States is interested in little except material values.

As important as this activity is, there is a more significant political aspect to the arts than "image-building" for the state. Art, in short, reminds us of our better nature in a world that too easily forgets and places the crises and torments of the moment in a larger perspective. It is mainly in these ways, rather than in the narrow propagandistic sense, that art makes its contribution to better relations between peoples.

Many social and political forces have combined, at this moment of history, both to compel interest in the arts and to justify that interest in practical terms. The intersection of these forces provides an unparalleled opportunity for the arts and the nation, particularly since it occurs at a moment when a surge of vitality in the arts themselves has brought their needs and their delights to the attention of the national consciousness as never before. Wisely applied, all these factors can lead to an environment more conducive to distinguished performance, to a larger and more appreciative audience, and to a higher level of artistic accomplishment.

This report is primarily intended to deal with the hard realities and the most practical solutions to the problems confronting only one area of artistic endeavor. Our study is limited to the *live performing* arts, and we concentrate on the *professional organizations* that sponsor and present opera, drama, instrumental and choral music, and dance. We do so because this is where the need is greatest and because the problems presented in the performing arts are uniquely susceptible to solution by public interest and action. These are, in effect, the public arts, those that can best be aided by the kind of broad discussion and institutional interest it is our hope to stimulate by this report.

Our choice of focus on the live performing arts is not due to any lack of appreciation of the importance of the performing arts presented electronically. On the contrary, we fully recognize that electronic devices—movies, television, radio, and recording—have a tremendous role to play in the development of the performing arts. But it is a role of such magnitude and complexity, so different in form, that it can be treated adequately only by a separate study, differently conceived and executed.

Our concentration on the professional performing arts bespeaks no disdain of the amateur and quasi-professional performing arts. We recognize that they can attain the highest level of artistic excellence, can provide fine entertainment, and can play a vital role in developing a larger and better audience for the arts. We do, however, feel it is on the professionals that we must primarily depend for the development and maintenance of high standards of artistic performance, which is a paramount concern.

We recognize that in the early stage of development many of our theatre groups, opera companies, symphony orchestras, and dance ensembles cannot attain the highest level of excellence. But if they are to thrive, aesthetically and economically, they should be aiming for the highest possible quality and be making perceptible progress in this direction. This is also a process that involves the standards of artistic taste of our audiences, which are first nurtured by the family, then developed by the educational system. It is a process that involves sharp disagreement over what constitutes distinguished artistic performance, even among those with imposing credentials as critics. This disagreement, however, is neither so broad nor so mysterious as to prevent rising standards of artistic quality within the terms each organization sets for itself.

This study's focus on organizations engaged in sponsoring and presenting the performing arts limits our attention primarily to *nonprofit* arts organizations because most of the sponsoring and presenting organizations are of this type. Here again, this does not reflect any disregard of the importance of the performing arts presented commercially. They obviously play a key role in the field as a whole and particularly in the theatre. Nor does our concentration on arts organizations involve any lack of concern for the financial plight of the great body of our performing artists as individuals. It merely reflects our basic conviction that if arts organizations can be strengthened, the increased strength will flow to the artists as well.

The organizations with which this study deals are as lively as the most lively artists. Any study dealing with them in static terms would be out of date before leaving the printer. So this study is one of motion and of trends. If it looks to the past, it is for clues to the future. It deals with possibilities and alternatives, and here and there with prophecy.

But one thing is immediately clear: The potential for successful development of the performing arts is tremendous. There are millions of Americans who have never seen a live professional performance or participated in a live performance of any kind. There are untold numbers who might, with opportunity and training, become first-rate performing artists. There are electronic devices, still in a relatively early stage of development, to bring performances to vast audiences at modest expense. And the material resources to do all these things are available if we choose to apply them.

Along with the possibilities, there is a risk that growth will be haphazard and shoddy, that the nation will drift along instead of meeting the challenge to make the performing arts the adventure they can be. Thus, despite the manifest opportunities that the arts today enjoy, much of the discussion in the following chapters will necessarily be critical.

The panel is motivated by the conviction that the arts are not for a privileged few but for the many, that their place is not on the periphery of society but at its center, that they are not just a form of recreation but are of central importance to our well-being and happiness. In the panel's view, this status will not be widely achieved unless artistic excellence is the constant goal of every artist and every arts organization, and mediocrity is recognized as the ever-present enemy of true progress in the development of the arts.

2
The Performing Arts—Today and Tomorrow

A tremendous expansion has taken place in the arts in this country in the past two decades. In the performing arts alone, observers note that:

> The recent total of 1,401 symphony orchestras is more than double the number existing in 1939.
>
> The 754 groups now presenting opera are almost twice the number so engaged a decade ago.
>
> Theatrical enterprises now number about 40,000 and have increased by about 15 percent in the last ten years.
>
> The number of dance companies has grown to a total approaching 200.

The amount of money paid for admissions to the performing arts, now running well above $400 million a year, has approximately doubled during the past decade and a half.

Next to this glowing picture must be placed another, more sobering one: *Almost all this expansion is amateur.* The American people may have experienced an extraordinary awakening to the performing arts, but comparatively few are ever exposed to any *live professional* presentations. By way of rough illustration:

Broadway, historically the creative center of the American theatre, has reduced its output from an average of 142 productions per year during the thirties to 63 in 1963–64, and its playhouses have diminished in number from 54 to 36 in the same span of years.

The number of commercial theatres in the country has dropped from 590 in 1927 to barely 200.

Of 1,401 symphony orchestras, only 54 are composed predominantly of professional musicians.

In the entire country there are only five or six dance companies that meet high professional standards and possess any real degree of institutional stability; only one approaches giving year-round performances.

Of the 754 opera-producing groups, only 35 to 40 are fully professional, and not more than 10 of these provide performances more than fifteen days in the year.

There is certainly nothing wrong with a strong amateur movement. To the contrary, amateur performing artists are a vital element in the audience for the professional arts, and their proselytizing devotion to the cause of culture is probably the principal reason that the audience for the performing arts has continued its steady growth in this country. The amateur movement also provides an opportunity for young people who will ultimately become professionals to gain their first experience, though its role in this regard is perhaps overstressed. Most important, many communities away from the great urban cultural centers would have no live performing arts at all were it not for the efforts of amateurs.

But vital to our cultural health as the amateurs are, the fact remains that it is on the professional performing artists and arts organizations that ultimate responsibility for the highest levels of creative output and quality rests. Some of these organizations, particularly the orchestras, are expanding rapidly, some are actually in declining health, others are just barely holding their own, and others are growing at a rate much slower than might be. In general, there has been no significant improvement in the basic health of the professional arts organizations. There is much to be done.

PROBLEMS IN COMMON

In the broadest possible terms, the task before the professional performing arts organizations is the consolidation of the growth that has already taken place and the continued extension of that growth, perhaps at a still faster pace. This, in turn, means there is need for the creation of new organizations of two types. A wide variety of service and information organizations is necessary to collect statistics, to provide guidance on the general direction of growth and change, and to bring together those responsible for the direction of arts organizations to exchange ideas about the solutions for common problems.

More organizations devoted to the presentation of the arts are also required. Here, there is need for experiment. There are today large population centers that lack adequate facilities for the presentation of the arts or—much worse—lack the dance or opera or theatre company that would add a significant dimension to their cultural lives. In the long run, it is essential to encourage formation of resident organizations. In the meantime, there is perhaps more pressing need for regional organizations designed specifically to serve large geographic areas. There are many population centers that are incapable of sponsoring full-time arts organizations alone, but together they could support a first-class organization, making limited tours and playing short seasons throughout the area.

Touring organizations, specially created to bring stimulating artistic presentations to every area of the country, could have a profound effect on our standards of excellence. These organizations would be quite different from the commercial theatrical ventures, which are our usual models when we discuss "the road." They should be permanent companies with continuity of management and, as far as possible, performers; they must take full advantage of modern transportation and new production techniques that, properly utilized, can lower the cost of touring; and they must have a stable financial base, unlike the dance companies for instance, which now take rather desperately and haphazardly to the road in search of audiences. There is no need to gloss over the difficulties inherent in suggesting an intermediate push toward regional companies. One of the greatest roadblocks will be the difficulty of developing individual community enthusiasm and support for nonresident organizations.

However, as will be stressed time and again in this report, the extension of cooperative efforts to solve the common problems of the arts and the creation of new, carefully planned and well-financed arts organizations, some of which will attempt a new type of touring, are both basic to improving the condition of the performing arts in this country. Indeed, many of the specific problems, to which we now turn, would be well on their way to solution if this kind of basic expansion were undertaken.

Poverty for the Professional. Most performing artists are poorly paid, a fact dramatically documented in the congressional hearings in 1961 and 1962 on economic conditions in the performing arts. The miserable income of the majority reflects both a shortage of jobs and the brief duration of employment that is available. In all except the small handful of our major and metropolitan orchestras, the musicians earn an average of only a few hundred dollars a year from their professional labors. During an average week in the winter season, only about one-fifth of the active members of Actors' Equity Association, the theatrical performers union, are employed in the profession. Of the actors who do find jobs, well over half are employed for only ten weeks—less than one-fifth of the year. For most opera companies the season lasts only a few weeks. The livelihood of the dancer is perhaps the most meager of all.

In addition to low income, short seasons, and the general scarcity of employment opportunities, the performing artist—and the musician in particular—must often meet out of his salary heavy costs for travel, equipment and instruments, agent's fees, lessons, and other professional expenses. He often finds himself ineligible for social security and unemployment insurance benefits. Far too many artists must still rely for the major portion of their income on employment not connected with the arts. Quality of performance is inevitably subjected to severe strains as a result of this vicious circle of inadequate pay and limited opportunity.

Second-Class Training. If the performing arts are to fulfill their cultural mission in the United States, marked improvement in the quality of the training of professional artists will be required. It has been authoritatively asserted that much of the dance instruction available in this country is harmful aesthetically and, frequently, harmful physically as well. In the theatre there is widespread complaint of ill-trained craftsmanship on the part of those seeking professional status.

The symphony orchestra field affords a striking illustration of the need to relate training to needs. At present there is an acute shortage of well-trained stringed instrument players for orchestras. A part of the explanation seems to lie in the attention paid by high schools, colleges, and universities to marching and concert bands. More and better training of string players is essential to the development of high orchestral proficiency.

A Place to Perform. Despite the pioneering development of Lincoln Center for the Performing Arts in New York and the number of fine modern theatres that have been built by universities and civic groups for resident companies, physical facilities for the performing arts as a whole remain woefully inadequate. No new theatre has been built on Broadway since 1928—significantly, the year when talking movies were introduced—and those surviving from that era are almost uniformly antiquated. For halls in which to practice and perform, most opera, dance, and choral groups are regularly compelled to rely on poorly adapted school and civic auditoriums or similarly ill-suited structures.

Testifying to the previous lack of facilities as well as to the present widespread public interest in the arts is the fact that more than one hundred "cultural centers" are being built or planned in communities throughout the country. Only about thirty of these are true arts centers, specifically designed to accommodate more than one performing art; many are merely sports arenas and convention halls that can house a cultural presentation only inadequately. Nevertheless, even thirty arts centers represent welcome progress, provided both the buildings and the programs of cultural presentations are carefully planned in advance.

Sponsoring Organizations. It is characteristic of the performing arts that outstanding success can almost always be traced to some gifted, inspired, and driving individual. Organizations can provide no substitute for this individual effort. But they can give it an underpinning.

Indeed, the lack of development and stability of the performing arts is frequently due to the absence of strong sponsoring organizations. For example, there has been expansion of both performance and audience for the dance. But with very few exceptions, the expansion has not been attended by the development of sustaining organizations to provide the essential stability, continuity, and financial support. Much the same is true of operatic and choral groups, and until very recently of theatre.

Curse of "Crisis Financing." There are relatively few performing arts organizations that do not leap from deficit to deficit in Eliza-like fashion as they struggle to continue their activities. Although nonprofit corporations do not aspire to make a profit but simply to balance income and expenditure, they have not found this easy to do in spite of the expanding "market." Even the most permanent and venerable organizations have, almost without exception, increasing fiscal problems. Their continuing financial trials and tribulations forcibly raise the question of the extent to which the box office can and should be relied upon to pay the way of the performing arts.

Planning and Research—Neglected Resources. Because of their preoccupation with immediate problems of solvency, most arts organizations have had little chance to study their long-range goals in the community and the means for achieving them. In addition, pertinent information about such matters as audience composition and tastes is rarely available. Even fewer organizations have undertaken to explore systematically what the continuing scientific revolution—reflected in changes in such things as lighting, color projection, and the transmission of sound—can mean for the technological improvement of their artistic endeavors and for the strengthening of their economic sinews. Imaginative and well-directed research would not only make it possible to present the performing arts in their traditional forms more effectively and possibly more inexpensively than at present but could also lead to new and aesthetically exciting forms. The performing arts have perforce been laggard in sharing in the research revolution.

In order to understand how these common problems and opportunities are being faced today and what trends are discernible toward a more productive future it is necessary to examine each art separately.

SYMPHONY ORCHESTRAS

Of all existing professional organized activity in the performing arts, the longest established, most widely dispersed, and most stable is the symphony orchestra. Partly because of the prestige that accompanies experience and age (the New York Philharmonic was founded in 1842, the Boston Symphony Orchestra in 1881), partly because of the increased exposure given to music by radio, recordings, and television, American orchestras today occupy an eminent position in our cultural life.

Of the 1,401 symphony orchestras in the United States, 288 are college and university orchestras, adjuncts to music departments; 1,059 are community orchestras operating on budgets of less than $100,000 a year, most of whose members are musicians by avocation. Of the 60,000 persons playing regularly, only about 7,200 are professional. The concert seasons of the community orchestras range from one or two performances a year to as many as forty. Although they are often under professional leadership and sometimes achieve a high level of quality, they are roughly equivalent to community theatres where amateurs predominate.

Of the remaining fifty-four orchestras, twenty-nine are usually referred to as metropolitan orchestras. At present the metropolitan orchestras' annual budgets range from $100,000 to $386,000. Some are made up entirely of professional musicians, in others the membership is a mixture of professional and amateur performers. Of some 2,200 players in the metropolitan orchestras, 80 percent are professionals.

The twenty-five remaining orchestras are the so-called major orchestras, all of whose musicians are professional. Their annual budgets all exceed $278,000, and rise, in the case of the three largest—the Philadelphia, New York, and Boston orchestras—to between $2 million and $2.75 million. Each major and metropolitan orchestra presents a regularly scheduled series of public concerts; each is an established civic institution with a board of directors, a supporting public, a professional conductor—and an operating deficit. The distinction between the categories of orchestras is based entirely on the size of annual budgets —reflecting length of season and scope of operation—not on a judgment of artistic merit.

Despite their place in the community and the support they receive, most major and metropolitan symphony orchestras have serious problems and face a far from secure future. For the vast majority of the approximately four thousand musicians who play in them, full-time symphonic employment is unknown. It is true that year-round contracts are or will soon be in effect for the Philadelphia, Boston, New York, and Cleveland orchestras. But the seasons of the twenty-one other major organizations range from twenty-two to forty weeks. The average salary per orchestra ranges from $2,000 to $9,000. Their musicians generally must find outside employment in music or another field. The plight of members of metropolitan orchestras is even less happy. Their seasons of employment are still shorter—from sixteen to thirty-one weeks—and their need for other employment even greater than for members of the majors.

The idea of the orchestra as purveyor of musical services—a musical talent organization providing the musicians for an assortment of activities—is attracting study as one solution to some of the orchestra's basic problems. The experience of the Milwaukee Symphony (an orchestra in the metropolitan category) illustrates how an organization can expand its services to the community and effectively assist its musicians. Sixty-five of the orchestra's seventy-seven members are retained on weekly salary (though not throughout the year), and their services used in smaller ensembles—twenty-piece, forty-piece, and sixty-piece groups, as well as in trios, quartets, and quintets of both strings and woodwinds. By aggressive promotion, new audiences and support for the services of these groups, as well as for the full orchestra, have been developed throughout Wisconsin. Four banks, for example, have sponsored appearances of the full orchestra in smaller communities. While this kind of sponsorship does not meet full costs, the concerts have stirred up a statewide sense of pride in the orchestra and increased private and business patronage. The city of Milwaukee extends support in the form of a $40,000 appropriation for the purchase of services from the orchestra, and both the University of Wisconsin and Marquette University are arranging concert series by the full orchestra. As a result of all these efforts, the 1964–65 season increased from twenty-eight weeks to thirty-two weeks.

The Honolulu Symphony Orchestra is an example of a metropolitan orchestra that travels to its audience. Faced with the unique challenge of operating in widely dispersed areas, it literally takes to the air to provide music throughout the islands. George Barati, its conductor for the past fifteen years, believes music is important to people no matter what the conditions under which it must be played—a burning sun, a windstorm, in small or large halls. If the buildings do not exist he plays anyway, believing that if people can hear, eventually they will demand proper facilities.

Because of the superior organization and stability of symphony orchestras, they might well become the keystone in a developing arch of cooperative performing arts endeavors. Neither opera nor ballet can properly exist without an orchestra; opera generally needs dancers and a chorus as well. Using the orchestra as the basic component, these other forms might be created around it.

The symphony might be the orchestra for both opera and dance, thereby extending its own season and removing the need for a separate orchestra for the other two arts. It also can help build the season for a professional chorus and initiate chamber groups of its own members. Cooperation could make possible more chamber opera, light opera, and opera in concert form.

Herbert Graf, an authority on opera, notes that many symphonies are already presenting operas in concert form. If a community orchestra gives twelve programs a year, he suggests that perhaps two of them might consist of fully staged operas, with costumes and scenery. Included in the symphony's subscription series, these performances could be a first step toward introducing a community to the pleasures of opera and awakening interest in expanding a season to the point where it would be practical to consider forming an opera company as a department of the symphony.

It is possible to look realistically toward the day when cooperative ventures involving the orchestras and all the arts, in every conceivable combination, will supply some of the solutions to the most crucial problems that now face them.

CHORAL MUSIC

More Americans—the number is probably in the millions—participate in organized choral singing than in any other performing art, but there is less organized professional activity here than in any other phase of music.

There are no year-round professional choruses anywhere in the country. Only a small number of singers, in a handful of cities, consider themselves professional choristers, and even these sing under a variety of sponsors; the turnover is rapid, and there is no permanence to the profession. Few choral institutions exist outside the church, the high school, the university, and the opera company.

Although choral music had its origin in the church, only the wealthier churches hire professional choirs. Elsewhere, amateur singers predominate, often supplemented by professional soloists. There are a few truly professional secular choruses; each chorister is a trained vocalist receiving union scale wages for rehearsals and performances, and the chorus is conducted by a professional musician. Among the best known are the De Paur Chorus, the Gregg Smith Singers, the Karlsrud Chorale, the Norman Luboff Choir, the Robert Shaw Chorale, the Roger Wagner Chorale, and the Schola Cantorum. None of these is in any sense a year-round organization able to provide its members with an adequate income.

In addition, there are the opera choruses of the Metropolitan Opera, the New York City Opera, the San Francisco and Chicago operas, and several smaller groups. Ordinarily all these groups use professional singers, but except for the Metropolitan Opera Chorus, their seasons are short. Most other opera choruses in the country are *ad hoc* collections of singers with no real group identity. Only one symphony, the Chicago, has its own professional chorus.

At present then, amateur choral activity predominates. While in many instances it is of near-professional quality, the fact is that much of the finest choral repertory requires professional skill for its fullest realization. Thus, there is an essential artistic need for the professional chorus, but it faces a difficult struggle to gain public acceptance and support.

To improve this situation, nonprofit professional choruses might be established in several regions, under first-rate conductors, with a guaranteed season and adequate financing. The choruses could give concerts on their own and be available for radio and television appearances. They could tour their region both alone and in company with an orchestra, opera, or ballet company.

These choruses should be organized in the same way as the symphony orchestras, soliciting funds from the public. From all indications there would be enough opportunities for at least one group in each of as many as six regions to be occupied full time. Establishment of these choruses could go far toward putting the art of choral singing on a sound professional footing and create valuable pace setters for the best of the community, university, and conservatory choruses.

CHAMBER MUSIC

The growth of interest in chamber music, both professional and amateur, in the last forty years has equaled, if not exceeded, orchestral and operatic development, but this has not as yet been translated into any kind of stable organizational structure. Few chamber ensembles are set up on a nonprofit, tax-exempt basis. For this reason, support from philanthropic or government sources is virtually excluded unless a cultural or educational institution is willing to serve as middleman or host. This is indeed happening. More than a hundred colleges and universities now maintain chamber groups in residence for part or all of the academic year, performing and teaching in the region.

The difficulties facing the development of permanent, full-season chamber groups are formidable. The character of the music generally dictates the use of a small hall, and although the fee commanded by even the best established string quartet is far less than that paid a famous soloist, it is generally high in relation to potential box office receipts. On the other hand, the moderate cost of presenting chamber music and the relative mobility of its practitioners make it comparatively simple to arrange wide tours. As a result, greater demand and better economic conditions for the performers should develop naturally. Another promising avenue of development, already mentioned, is the promotion of chamber groups by the less-than-full-season symphony orchestras. Support from that source, plus the growing sponsorship by universities, might provide the needed institutional stability and financial strength for this often neglected form of musical activity.

OPERA

Of all the performing arts, grand opera can clearly be the most spectacular, the most aristocratic, and the most expensive. With a full orchestra, chorus, and ballet, with great divas and supporting artists, with huge productions and sizable repertory, a grand opera company can stand in majestic solitude, dwarfing by sheer magnitude dramas and musical comedies, orchestras both symphonic and chamber, and even ballet.

There are few opera houses in the world that boast a greater roster of big name performers, a more sumptuous setting, a more devoted following, a greater outpouring of money (over $9 million projected for 1964–65), than New York's Metropolitan Opera. But with the exception of three other major companies—the New York City Opera, the Chicago Lyric Opera, and the San Francisco Opera—plus two or three young and special operatic enterprises, the United States has little or no professional opera during most of the year. Indeed, it can reasonably be questioned whether opera is given any appreciable firsthand exposure to the American people as a whole. For millions it is looked upon as the special responsibility of the rich and the socially prominent; as a scarce commodity known to most people only through Saturday afternoon radio broadcasts that reward the ear but leave the eye untouched.

There is, to be sure, another side to this picture. In the 1963–64 season alone, there were 754 opera-producing organizations in the country, 227 of these within the music departments of our universities. A total of 3,877 performances of 321 different works was presented. Thousands of Americans are participating in opera, either as performers or as audience. But, as in the other performing arts, most of this grassroots development is amateur, and there is little cross-fertilization between these groups and professional opera. A great proportion of the young singers who have been trained have no professional outlet in this country. At the moment, indeed, some five to six hundred young Americans are trying to gain the professional experience abroad that they cannot find at home.

Of the 754 opera-producing groups, only 35 to 40 are in the fullest sense professional, and the great majority of these offer engagements for artists during seasons that run less than twenty-five performances annually. The only exceptions are the four major companies mentioned above, plus the Santa Fe and Central City summer operas and the Boris Goldovsky touring company. But how can a stable and continuing opera program be developed, an ensemble and orchestra be maintained, individual singers be supported, permanent public interest be organized, when for 340 days of the year no professional opera exists in such major cities as Boston, Cincinnati, Dallas, Hartford, Houston, Kansas City, New Orleans, Philadelphia, Pittsburgh, or Washington?

The answer for the cities that do undertake a limited professional opera season (and all those just mentioned do) is to import talent on a transient basis. Opera singers at all levels, even including the great stars, travel about from place to place, singing for a few nights in an ensemble framework that is largely improvised. In some cities, the engagement of a Tebaldi, a Sutherland, or a Callas is the only thing that insures a season at all.

Another characteristic of the opera world today is its widespread devotion to established tradition: the standard works, the known names, the accepted look. Opera managements in this country are notable for their reluctance to perform new works, to engage unknown singers for key roles, to experiment with fresh styles. For the opera companies offering very limited seasons, works from the standard repertory are required by economics, both of audience acceptance and production requirements. For the established companies, from the Metropolitan down, the rationale is twofold. First, every musically developed country must have its national custodian of the classical repertory to maintain standards of performance and give young artists a focus for their aspirations. Second, as in symphonic programing, this seems to be what the public wants, and box office figures seem to support this position. Public taste is indeed conservative. Unlike theatregoers, for whom the new play exerts more attraction than the revival, the musical public seems chary of new works and clings to the established favorites. But preoccupation with past glory contributes little to the vitality of opera as a living art form. No one believes we should turn our back on the great heritage of operatic literature, from Mozart to Wagner and Verdi; neither, however, can opera fulfill its role in America if its predominant interest continues to be in the eighteenth and nineteenth centuries. After all, we are already two-thirds of the way through the twentieth. It is very simply part of responsible management to encourage the public at least to sample the adventure of the new.

Remedies for these problems exist and in some places may be observed in practice. The Metropolitan has presented several contemporary works in recent years. More active in this respect is the New York City Opera, which, aided by Ford Foundation grants, has produced thirty-one contemporary works since 1957—more than any other opera company in the world—and it received, in June 1964, a further grant of $250,000 to help make possible spring seasons of contemporary opera in 1965 and 1966, with at least six different works to be offered each season. The Santa Fe Opera, which presents a summer season of nine weeks, usually includes two or three contemporary works (Alban Berg's "Lulu" received its American premiere there in 1963). It also offers one or two older but rarely done operas, which makes a very fair balance with the standard repertory. The Kansas City Lyric Theatre in 1963 collaborated with the University of Kansas City in presenting a spring season of American works. The Opera Society of Washington also seeks a balance between old and new: Barber, Hindemith, and Schönberg are offered along with Mozart, Puccini, and Verdi. Opera in concert form has long been a method of production that lends itself to use by community and university groups because of its relative simplicity and economy. Several professional groups have been offering concert opera series annually in New York in recent years and have been the vehicle for the introduction of rarely heard opera of earlier periods and contemporary works.

The twentieth century does then occasionally push its way onto the stages of a few American opera houses. And the voices of young professionals are occasionally heard in major roles in some places. The Metropolitan annually holds national auditions to recruit new members for its company, a number of whom have become leading artists of international standing (Leonard Warren, Eleanor Steber, Risë Stevens, Robert Merrill, Regina Resnik, and others). But it is the New York City Opera that provides greater opportunities for experience in the principal roles to which young artists aspire. Since its annual budget of approximately $800,000 is less than 10 percent of the Metropolitan's, and since its top ticket price is $4.95 against the latter's $13, it obviously cannot afford the great stars. Making a virtue of its relative poverty, the New York City Opera casts its productions with the best young singers it can find. The Spring Opera of San Francisco offers a six-week season performed entirely by young professionals. The Tebaldis and Callases find no place on the stages of the Washington and Kansas City opera houses either, and the leading roles there are sung instead by artists on their way up the ladder.

The basic problem is that of making opera performances of first-class professional caliber available to more people. The amount of amateur operatic activity indicates that there is a sizable potential audience for professional presentations, and the mounting of more professional operas would not only benefit this audience but also create more opportunities for the young professional singer.

The most satisfactory method may be the touring company. The Metropolitan has an annual spring tour, which will take it to eight cities in 1965. The cost of touring on the Met's scale is prodigious and its price scale remains beyond the means of the average man; its out-of-New York appearances have become geographically more limited as it has felt the pinch of rising costs. The New York City Opera toured fifteen cities in its home state in 1963 with support from the New York State Council on the Arts and performed in thirteen other cities in the eastern and midwestern states. The San Francisco Opera, with an extended season in Los Angeles, tours its neighboring region. All these tours are, however, peripheral to the main operations of these companies.

One professional company whose *raison d'être* is to tour is already in existence; another is just being formed. The Goldovsky Opera Theatre will bring opera to eighty-five American cities in 1964–65. To be sure, it is scaled-down, nonrepertory opera, with an orchestra of but twenty players, a small chorus, and uncomplicated sets whose core is a lightweight collapsible fiberglass shell. But it is judged to be opera of high quality, the result of long rehearsal in advance of the tour and of an excellent group of artists.

A permanent national company of the Metropolitan Opera will be inaugurated in the fall of 1965. Risë Stevens and Michael Manuel have been named general managers, and funds are being raised (an estimated $1.2 million will be needed for its five-year launching period). Plans for the first season include a thirty-five-week tour of some sixty communities, playing 245 performances, with a repertory of four operas and a company of singers, dancers, and musicians numbering 125.

Neither Goldovsky's present nor the Metropolitan's future touring companies will solve the problem alone, but they point the way. One can envisage a day when the New York City Opera and the Chicago and San Francisco operas can expand their touring, for none provides anything like full-season employment for its artists; a day when other regionally established professional operas will be able to sustain themselves by touring throughout their areas. To accomplish this it will be necessary to set up companies realistically financed and based on the excellence of the entire company rather than merely on the drawing power of transient guest stars. This will doubtless take a long time, much of it devoted to re-education of the public. But it is the only way opera can become a meaningful experience to more than a handful of our citizens.

THEATRE

In the theatre, a process of reorientation and reorganization is already underway, altering the theatrical structure as it has existed.

The theatre is the only performing art that has flourished as a commercial enterprise and been thought of as capable of self-support. But in fact the commercial theatre has been shrinking—on Broadway, on the road, and in local stock companies. Broadway has been the center for which our finest playwrights have written, in which our greatest performing talents have flourished, from which our American stage has taken its creative direction. With a yearly investment of approximately $10 million in new productions, Broadway has in effect provided the experimental laboratory for drama in the United States. As a profitmaker it has become a dubious venture. About 75 percent of the plays produced fail to make money. However, the profit motive can still be very strong because a hit can provide a substantial financial gain to its backers.

Broadway's output has dwindled from an average of 142 productions per year during the thirties to 63 in 1963–64. Outside New York the shrinkage has been comparable. Theatres that thirty years ago housed prosperous local professional stock companies and touring road shows have been turned into movie houses or torn down. Because of its anarchic organization, laissez-faire individualism, and transient character, the commercial theatre has barely survived the competition of the mass media and a constant increase in production and operating costs without a comparable increase of revenues. Its difficulties have also been aggravated by some questionable methods employed in the distribution of tickets and some dubious business practices in the financing of productions.

Since 1964, however, producers wishing to raise money have been required by law to reveal profits and losses on previous productions and to estimate how much money must be grossed if backers are to be returned their original investment. In addition, responding to public criticism, the League of New York Theatres and the Shubert Theatrical Enterprises are undertaking a study, to be completed in 1965. This action may lead to a major overhaul of Broadway. The appointment of a commissioner empowered to take action to improve the condition of the commercial theatre, as well as to enforce codes of ethical practices, will be considered. This study, involving an extraordinary degree of cooperation where there has been very little, could have a substantial revitalizing effect on the Broadway theatre.

In any event, no one expects Broadway to collapse. It will continue to provide entertainment of high quality. But Broadway as we knew it—the Broadway for which every major playwright from O'Neill to Miller and Williams has principally written, the Broadway that has provided stardom for hundreds of major talents from Ethel Barrymore to Ethel Merman—is being challenged, its audiences are turning elsewhere. It is, in fact, being bypassed by those who wish to offer and those who wish to accept the theatre as one of America's flourishing art forms. It is this process that has most significance today.

One need not leave New York City to find the evidence. In 1943, the New York City Center of Music and Drama came into being as a nonprofit organization to provide a stage for opera, dance, musical comedy, and, on occasion, drama. Aided through virtual remission of rent on its city-owned 3,000-seat house, each of its semi-autonomous units has cooperated in keeping ticket prices well below the Broadway level—the top is now $4.95—and it enjoys a large and devoted following.

Other nonprofit theatrical enterprises have followed the City Center. In 1953, the Phoenix Theatre was founded. Dedicated to a varied program of classical, musical, and new works—also offered at less than Broadway prices—it presented some seventy-five productions in its first decade. The New York Shakespeare Festival has maintained allegiance to the idea of *free* theatre ever since it was organized in 1954. Now occupying an outdoor playhouse built specially for it in Central Park, it was receiving by the early sixties sizable grants from the city of New York and recurring support from foundations and individual donors. In 1962, the Actors Studio, originally created as an advanced training program for experienced actors, formed a producing company of its own members. Already a nonprofit educational organization, it looked upon this expansion of its work as leading toward an institutional theatre.

The objective of the Repertory Theatre of Lincoln Center, which opened in 1963, has been widely publicized: to form a permanent acting company that occupies a permanent home and presents in repertory both new plays and revivals. It represents the most costly undertaking yet tried in America to create an organization similar to the great theatre companies of Europe. One of the most notable aspects of its first season was the participation of two of America's best playwrights, Arthur Miller and S. N. Behrman. If more arrangements can be made for our finest dramatists to be produced outside the framework of Broadway, a major step will have been taken toward the building of a new pattern for serious theatre in this country.

The off-Broadway movement is another significant part of the bypassing of Broadway. In little more than a decade and a half, it has grown until it has more playhouses than Broadway, although most of them seat less than three hundred. In 1963–64, it presented ninety-one productions—outproducing Broadway by more than one-third.

Off-Broadway has made several major contributions to the New York theatrical scene. It has served as a showcase for young talent—acting and directing. It has developed some of the finest young American playwrights—Edward Albee, for example. It has provided New Yorkers with many opportunities for exposure to the European avant-gardists—Beckett, Ionesco, Genet, and Pinter. It has offered the literature of the theatre on its stages by producing the great works of the past from Euripides to O'Neill. It has kept alive recent works of merit by such American dramatists as Williams, Miller, and Wilder. Finally, it has brought ticket prices down to a level that can be afforded by an audience naturally attracted to these works.

Most off-Broadway producers—even those who are strongly noncommercial in their motivations and choice of material—have sought to operate for commercial profit. If the present pattern continues—rising costs, increasing ticket prices—they are likely to become prone to the same anarchic tendencies and uncertainties as the Broadway they sought to combat and will be as hard to help as the rest of the commercial theatre. The 1964–65 season began ominously with far fewer new productions scheduled than in the previous year and with some theatre owners taking steps to convert their houses to other uses.

The bypassing process—the development of nonprofit organizations and commercial enterprises outside the Broadway framework—is not the only radical change in the structure of the theatre. The second alteration in the picture since midcentury is the beginning of the decentralization of high-quality professional theatre throughout the country. For years, observers concerned with the health and growth of the stage have been asking: If many of our cities could support professional symphony orchestras, could they not support professional theatres too? The obvious answer has been that they could if they wanted to, but there was not sufficient demand. Now we see the beginning of a demand, and we see steps taken to meet it.

There are some fifty permanent professional theatres operating today, more than half of them having been established since 1960—seven opening or turning professional during the 1964–65 season alone, most of them located outside New York City.* In 1964, Actors' Equity Association set up a department to respond to requests for assistance in the development of professional theatre throughout the country, appropriated $25,000 for the first year and appointed an executive director to implement the program.

More than half the professional theatre projects outside New York—and almost all the major ones—have been created as nonprofit undertakings. They share with Lincoln Center, the Phoenix, City Center, Actors Studio, and the Shakespeare Festival in New York the objective of serving their communities as cultural, not commercial, institutions.

In 1960, the Ford Foundation made grants to four of these theatres. One of them, the Phoenix, was in New York; but the others were in Washington (Arena Stage), San Francisco (Actor's Workshop), and Houston (Alley Theatre). All had been in existence for several years and had exhibited staying power; all had been trying to become stable institutions; all had need of support beyond the box office to enable them to grow, to establish permanent companies, and to develop community support.

Satisfied with its 1960 program, the Foundation in 1962 announced grants totaling $6 million to eight exist-

* By "permanent professional theatres" we mean those having management and policy continuity, playing extended seasons, generally of twenty weeks or more. The terms "resident theatre," "regional theatre," and "repertory theatre" have been used variously to describe the nonprofit permanent professional theatres outside of New York. We have chosen to avoid using these terms because they have been given such a wide variety of meanings and are not truly descriptive of all theatres that fall in the same category. A list of those presently existing is contained in the appendix.

ing theatre projects and one about to be created: to the Actors Studio in New York, the Actor's Workshop in San Francisco, the Alley Theatre in Houston, the Arena Stage in Washington, the Theatre Group of UCLA, the Milwaukee Repertory Theatre (formerly the Fred Miller Theatre), the Mummers Theatre in Oklahoma City, the American Shakespeare Festival Theatre and Academy at Stratford, Connecticut, and the Tyrone Guthrie Theatre in Minneapolis.

Many other permanent professional theatres have begun to take shape, often with the assistance of public or philanthropic groups. In Cincinnati, the city has made available for token rent a converted recreation building in a public park as a home for the Playhouse in the Park. The Seattle Repertory Theatre made its debut in the autumn of 1963 in a building erected for the World's Fair. Atlanta, Baltimore, Honolulu, Louisville, Philadelphia, and St. Paul all have nonprofit professional theatres recently established or shortly to open.

In contrast to the professional theatres being established in communities throughout the country, an example of decentralizing the theatre "on the road" must be noted. This is the company organized in 1961 and sent out by the nonprofit National Repertory Theatre Foundation. Headed by Eva Le Gallienne, it took three plays to fifteen cities across the country during the 1963–64 season, ending with a limited Broadway engagement. Its reception has been warm enough to indicate that many cities lacking permanent professional theatres of their own are anxious for serious drama, and those that have their own theatres are hungry for more.

There is a recent trend, too, toward strong university-theatre relationships. Many universities and colleges now accept a responsibility for cultural leadership extending to the performing arts. They often serve as impresarios in booking touring attractions, and there are three illustrations of professional theatre resident on the campus.

In 1959, the Theatre Group at UCLA was established under the sponsorship of the University's Extension Division and was given modest financial support. The project has grown and prospered and now looks forward to building a theatre of its own, enlarging its production schedule, and touring in the area.

Princeton University sponsors professional repertory at its McCarter Theatre, with the University guaranteeing the company against loss. In 1964–65, it housed the American Theatre Company. In addition, because of Princeton's proximity to the New York metropolitan area, the McCarter Theatre has adopted a highly successful policy of engaging Broadway and off-Broadway productions during their regular run on evenings when they are not playing in New York.

The Professional Theatre Program of the University of Michigan began in 1962–63 with the Association of Producing Artists (APA) in residence for a twenty-week annual season under a three-year contract. As part of the program, the University also provides professional internships for gifted theatre graduates from all over the country, has initiated a playwright-in-residence program under which an original play by a talented new playwright is produced, and presents a series of lectures on theatre by distinguished professionals.

Many summer projects involving professional performers have sprung up at universities since the war: at Antioch College, Brandeis University, the University of Denver, Stanford University—to cite a few. These companies use the facilities of the universities, and most are protected by them against loss.

Outdoor dramas celebrating the people and events of the nation's past have gained popularity in recent years and are often important tourist attractions. Local personnel and resources are generally relied on for financing, production, and performance. Some have had very long runs. "The Lost Colony" in North Carolina, for example, was first performed in the summer of 1937; "The Common Glory" in Virginia was given annually from 1947 to 1963, when it was replaced by "The Founders." Approximately twenty of these historical pageants and epic-dramas were presented during the summer of 1964.

Another summer phenomenon is the professional stock companies set up as profitmaking enterprises. Their continuing postwar increase—from 130 in 1948 to 151 in 1964—is another sign of decentralization. So are the thirty-five large, commercially successful musical theatres featuring revivals of successful Broadway musical comedies. The first of these was established in 1949 in Lambertville, New Jersey.

Then too, the community and amateur theatre movement in the United States has assumed large proportions. In 1964, there were approximately five thousand formal amateur theatre groups having some continuity of organization, while other groups, performing on varied schedules, were estimated at about thirty-five thousand. Performances vary enormously in quality, but some are good enough to compete vigorously with professional theatre.

All this activity demonstrates the broad appeal of the theatre in this country. It is a well-loved art form, and the one that may have the best possibility of quickly developing wide, new support, cutting across all social and cultural lines. The rise of the nonprofit permanent professional theatres is one of the most promising phenomena on the performing arts scene. They seem to point the way toward a long-awaited expansion of theatre—in both artistic and geographic terms.

In effect, the growth of the nonprofit professional playhouses represents an attempt to create a new theatrical structure to co-exist with the traditional commercial one. But it must not be imagined that the path to progress will be altogether smooth. Even after a theatre is organized it may take several years to take root in its community and to develop into an artistic unit of high quality.

Of course, foremost among the benefits of this theatrical expansion will be the increase of opportunities for actors. Through a survey in 1957–58 of nearly seven thousand of its members employed as performers, Actors' Equity Association estimated that the average actor's income approximated $2,000. Unquestionably, there will be more jobs available in the future with a resulting increase in income. However, many of these openings will be outside the major theatrical centers, forcing the actor to make a difficult decision. Seasons are sometimes too short to insure the actor an adequate livelihood, yet long enough to prevent his securing employment on Broadway, in films, or television. Walter Kerr, drama critic of the *New York Herald Tribune,* has written: "Generally, a sizable sacrifice is demanded of the actor, and if it is a sacrifice he would in his idealism be willing to make, it is frequently a sacrifice he does not dare to make, having mouths to feed."

The obvious solution is not only more theatres, but theatres with longer seasons. The exciting vision of lengthening seasons by having a company play in its own community for a regular season and then exchange visits with similar companies from other communities has, however, certain drawbacks. One is the basic incompatibility between the stages to which companies are accustomed. Some still work in traditional proscenium style theatres, others have chosen the currently fashionable thrust stages, still others work in the round. It is a difficult problem to solve, although adaptable stages can be designed.

In short, promising as are the developments in the theatre at the moment, it would be a mistake to believe that the current high pitch of excitement about them will carry everything before it. Thoughtful cooperation is needed now in order to coordinate the many new theatrical enterprises beginning in this country. We cannot afford to let unplanned development jeopardize the future of these organizations almost before they get started.

DANCE

From the standpoint of finance, administration, and organization, the dance world is close to chaos. There is only one theatre devoted exclusively to the dance—at Jacob's Pillow in Massachusetts, which is open only three months a year. At the moment not more than five or six dance companies can claim both a national reputation and a relatively stable institutional setup capable of surviving a crisis. There are also perhaps a dozen leading dancers, who scrape together companies, get up programs on shoestring budgets, and hope for a modest performance or two in New York, followed by a short and usually equally unprofitable road season. In this process there is little but toil and trouble for the choreographer as he scrimps and saves over long periods to enable himself to engage dancers, rehearse, rent a hall, and then put on a performance, the audience for which will probably consist of friends, a few admirers, a handful of *aficionados* of his form of the dance and, if he is lucky, one or two critics. Seldom, it might be said, has so much been done with so little for so few.

The public for dance—although growing steadily—probably does not approach a million regular attendants. It is concentrated in two or three large metropolitan areas, New York being by far the largest, with outposts at educational institutions that have strong dance departments. Indeed, these are the chief source of bookings for modern dance companies; without them, it seems safe to say, there would be no touring by American dancers. Even so, Martha Graham, the founder of modern dance in America, has not toured in her own country for fifteen years. It is just too hazardous economically.

If there is a relatively small public for the dance in America, this is in some measure due to the limited opportunities the average person has had to become acquainted with the art and to appreciate it. The mass media have been less well able to bring this art to a broad public than they have music and drama. Furthermore, the cost of touring, involving as it does not only soloists but a corps de ballet or an ensemble, plus musical accompaniment, is almost prohibitively high. Consequently, unless the potential dance enthusiast lives in one of the few centers that boasts a resident company, he has been denied anything but the most sporadic firsthand experience.

There are few fields of endeavor in the arts, however, that command the dedication that the world of dance receives from its participants and from those few who comprise its patrons and public. For the former there is negligible financial return: $3,000 to $3,500 a year is the average income for a professional dancer, and he would be fortunate if this were steady from year to year. A prima ballerina can today hope for no more than $10,000 a year from the practice of her art (by comparison, a great opera star can earn as much as $6,000 for a single performance). In 1964, the New York City Ballet became the first company in America to offer its dancers year-round employment; San Francisco, the next closest, provides about thirty-six weeks. Patrons, including Lincoln Kirstein, Lucia Chase, Jean Riddell, Ruth Page, and the B. de Rothschild and Rebekah Harkness foundations, have all but carried American dance on their shoulders for the past thirty years —that is, until the Ford Foundation joined them in 1963 by announcing grants totaling $7,756,000.

The Ford Foundation grants have understandably brought the whole dance field under new scrutiny, and this in itself has been useful. They have underlined the importance of George Balanchine, his aesthetic beliefs, his New York City Ballet, and its strong right arm, the School of American Ballet, since approximately $4.4 million of the Ford grants went to strengthen both company and school over a ten-year period. A program to improve instruction and performance in local communities received $1.5 million, and the rest of the grants have gone in varying amounts to the San Francisco Ballet, the National Ballet in Washington, and to companies in Boston, Houston, Philadelphia, and Salt Lake City.

Clearly the intent of the Ford Foundation grants has been to give massive support to a few established enterprises rather than spread itself more thinly over a larger number of less stable organizations. In making its selection, it has emphasized two factors: the importance of building a solid foundation and the importance of training. The level of American dance performance can be no higher than the level of its highly specialized and intensive training. But the haunting question continues to arise: training for what? America has far too few professional companies, and most of those that exist lead ephemeral lives, to say the least.

Let us consider briefly three outstanding dance organizations. The New York City Ballet is America's largest and most important dance institution. Its position is roughly comparable to the Metropolitan's in the field of American opera. Its 1962–63 season cost nearly $1.5 million, and it came within less than $50,000 of meeting those costs with the revenue from 223 performances given during its eleven-and-a-half-week season in New York plus seventeen weeks on tour. It is clearly a major and relatively successful operation, economically speaking.

The San Francisco Ballet is really two companies. The number one company dances thirteen weeks with the opera, gives ten performances of "The Nutcracker," has a three-week spring season and an eight-week national tour. The number two company has a short road tour of one-night stands in small cities and a summer season in which it performs new works. The Ballet also maintains a school, with an enrollment of 400 students, which gives recitals. This San Francisco pattern is one to be emulated.

Perhaps the most renowned modern dance company in the world is Martha Graham's. Due to the high cost of performing it is able to function only when presented by a government agency, a foundation, or some other interested agency or individual. At such times Miss Graham and members of her company are paid a fee by the presenting agency, which also pays the production expenses and covers the deficit a presentation inevitably entails. There is no profit or loss to the company, which exists only at these infrequent times of rehearsal and performance.

In addition to the few community-based companies, there are several dance groups, both classical and modern, that tour with varying degrees of success. The American Ballet Theatre travels for several weeks, in addition to an occasional brief New York season; the Chicago Opera Ballet performs in 80 to 115 cities yearly; José Greco tours practically year-round; and other dance companies, such as those led by Alvin Ailey, Merce Cunningham, Robert Joffrey, José Limon, and Paul Taylor, which have no permanent homes, travel to find audiences for their work.

In projecting the future pattern of dance in America, there is urgent need for encouragement of permanent companies that do exist and show potential for growth—encouragement toward stability within their own communities and encouragement to tour more widely than they are now able to do. The vitality of this art form, as of every other, depends as much upon the creation of new forms and contemporary expressions as upon the conservation of the heritage of the past. In other words, modern dance needs as much encouragement as classical ballet. Although attempts at cooperation in the dance world have met with little success, renewed efforts should be made to provide a permanent theatre in which several dance forms might be presented. Finally, the talented individuals who draw other talented dancers around them must appreciate the need for managerial support as well. If their creative work is to prosper, they should recognize that it must be accompanied by greater financial stability, that this can be acquired principally by organizational strength, that such organization need not be feared as a limit on artistic freedom but rather as an assurance of opportunities to create and perform.

THE WAY AHEAD

Over the last decade, some cities have begun construction of physical facilities that, properly used, have the potential of vastly increasing cooperative efforts in the arts and, ultimately, the audience for them. Others have experimented with community arts councils that carry out united fund drives for the arts, provide central services, and coordinate the efforts of the community's various artistic enterprises.

These developments are encouraging as manifestations of the recognition the arts have gained in many places in the United States. The new physical facilities, the arts centers, represent an attack on one of the oldest problems confronting the performing arts—the lack of suitable homes. In addition, it seems that the sharing of facilities within these new centers may lead, more or less naturally, to the sharing of talents in special performances, and perhaps, though this is much less certain, to entirely new art forms.

These arts centers, finally, could form the basis for regional and perhaps national networks of performing arts organizations. Until recently, the revival—let alone the expansion—of the road was a vain dream. There simply were not enough decent stages for the arts in this country. The new arts centers could change that and perhaps would even encourage the growth of new organizations specifically designed to tour or, at least, to spend more time away from their home bases. Surely the Metropolitan Opera, long beset by problems when its company went on the road each spring, would not be planning a new national touring company unless it saw in the existing and planned cultural centers the possibility of plenty of suitable homes away from home.

As the rise of new facilities encourages hope, so does the rise of other forms of cooperation between arts organizations. If arts councils in cities and states can focus attention on common problems and bring the representatives of various art forms together to help solve them, then it is possible to hope that these efforts can be expanded to embrace regional and national cooperative efforts.

The future, of course, must be one in which the performing arts are no longer part-time occupations, in which arts organizations provide their artists, as most now do not, with twelve-month employment and the public with year-round performances. It must also be a future in which the arts are available to all who desire them, regardless of the accidents of geographic location. With the partial exception of symphony orchestras, all the performing arts are still limited geographically to a few affluent urban centers. But we can scarcely be satisfied that our four or five finest orchestras lie east of the Mississippi, our two principal opera and ballet companies are 3,000 miles apart, and fine theatre is offered in scarcely more than a dozen cities.

Performing arts of high quality are costly, but relative to the wealth of our nation a decidedly modest financial outlay is all that is required for a broad extension of the opportunities to enjoy them. ***The panel recommends that the artistic goal of the nation be the day when the performing arts are considered a permanent year-round contribution to communities throughout the country, and our artists are considered as necessary as our educators.***

This, of course, is a long-term goal. In the view of the panel, a worthy interim objective for the nation would be the development and maintenance of the following high-quality nonprofit professional organizations operating on a year-round basis:

Fifty permanent theatre companies—a number approximating the metropolitan areas with populations over 500,000, a size large enough to support a year-round resident theatre.

Fifty symphony orchestras—presenting concerts by the full orchestra as well as providing musicians for smaller orchestral and chamber music groups.

Six regional opera companies—offering short seasons in several metropolitan areas not yet ready to support year-round performances—in addition to the four major resident companies and two permanent national touring companies already established.

Six regional choral groups.

Six regional dance companies, in addition to the two major resident dance groups now in existence.

There is obviously room for substantial differences in estimating the cost of such a nationwide performing arts establishment. Much would depend on the quality of the management, which is an element of decisive importance, the vigor of the promotional effort, and the degree of co-operation that could be attained between parts of the establishment—choral groups working with opera companies and symphony orchestras, for example. The best available estimates indicate that the amount currently being spent on running high-quality nonprofit professional performing arts organizations—which are now, in most cases, part-time operations—approximates $60 million. (It needs to be emphasized that this figure does not include the commercial theatre or the semiprofessional and amateur artistic activity in the country.) Well-informed estimates of the annual operating cost of the establishment outlined for the future fall between $150 million and $200 million (in current dollars). Therefore, somewhere between $90 million and $140 million of additional operating funds would be needed to put a professional performing arts establishment of the sort envisaged on a year-round basis of operation.

Arts organizations in the formative stages do less well at the box office than those that have had an opportunity to develop an audience, and some require a longer development time than others. Percentages of what can realistically be expected from the box office also vary from one performing art to another. But assuming that receipts will continue to constitute the same percentage they do now, between $50 million and $80 million annually could ultimately be expected to come from the sale of tickets at the box office. It follows that the new support required to meet the normal operating expenses of a professional performing arts establishment of the type indicated could be expected to be somewhere between $40 million and $60 million annually.* The larger amount is not much over one-hundredth of 1 percent of the nation's present annual income.

There is no intention here to suggest that the creation of the organizations and physical facilities essential to a performing arts program worthy of the United States is a slight undertaking. On the contrary, a vast amount of hard and intelligent work will be required. At the same

* These estimates are based on current costs and do not take into account capital expenditures for more and better halls and theatres, which will surely be necessary.

time there is no occasion for discouragement. Attainment of the ideal of giving all Americans the opportunity to share in the pleasures and rewards of the performing arts is no idle dream. It is easily within the capabilities of the nation.

3
Box Office and Other Earned Income

For almost all performing arts organizations the only major source of earned income is the sale of admission tickets for performances. For some organizations the sale of package performances to other organizations provides substantial receipts, and a few organizations of the very top artistic rank earn part of their income by performances for recording and broadcasting. Incidentals such as program advertising and concessions of various sorts are sometimes a minor source of earned income, generally running from 1 to 5 percent. But it is the box office (including the sales of season subscription tickets) that is the primary source of earned income.

BOX OFFICE

In considering the broad problem of financial support, the first question is: Why can't the sale of tickets pay all of the costs; if they have such an important cultural contribution to make, why can't the performing arts be self-sustaining?

The answer is complicated, filled with variables, and no single rule applies to all the arts or to all arts organizations. *But this panel believes that as a general principle the nonprofit performing arts organizations should not be expected to pay their way at the box office. Indeed, they cannot do so and still fulfill their true cultural mission. This does not mean that box office income cannot be improved or costs cut even as artistic and public obligations are met. On the contrary, every effort should be made to increase operating efficiency.*

The success of an artistic venture cannot be measured by the sale of tickets alone. To do so would be to submit to the tyranny of the box office, to surrender the right to fail and the right to experiment. All art cannot be forced into the position of having an overriding objective of instantaneous appeal to the widest possible audience for immediate commercial success. We have seen this aim in practice lay a restraining hand on the artistic development of films and television and, indeed, of Broadway.

Analogy to Higher Education

The role of the box office in supporting nonprofit arts organizations is roughly analogous to the role of tuition charges in providing financial support for colleges and universities. Even if it were possible to meet all educational costs in this way, such a course would be rejected. If tuition were raised to the point where it covered all costs, the broad diffusion of higher education would be impossible.

Similarly, box office prices are a compound of what *can* be and what *should* be. They are a compound that varies in degree from one performing art to another, from one community to another, and from one time to another. Hence, an almost infinite number of variables accounts for the inability of the box office to meet costs in any given case, but the outcome is remarkably consistent—the box office will pay only part of the costs.

Obligations of Nonprofit Organizations

A nonprofit performing arts organization first faces the problem of what it *can* feasibly collect at the box office. In dealing with this problem, it has the obligation to manage its operations as efficiently as possible. Indeed, there is no reason why the business operations of a nonprofit organization should not be as expertly managed as those of any profit-seeking organization. Better management will be reflected in better returns at the box office.

But even if a strictly economic or financial calculation were to show that the box office could be made to pay all the costs, the nonprofit arts organization would still have the problem of determining whether or not this course *should* be followed. Its obligations to its art and community might be poorly served by taking what the traffic would bear at the box office. These obligations include:

Maintaining the highest possible standards of performance.
Serving the community as broadly as possible.

Doing its best to protect and perpetuate the finest in its artistic heritage.

Developing new and experimental works.

Maintaining educational programs.

Providing opportunities for new talent.

Some Limiting Factors

In actual practice there is usually little conflict between the *can* and the *should* in establishing the fact that the box office will pay only a part of the costs of a nonprofit organization. In most instances, no matter what the policy, costs would still not be covered. The binding economic limits often are one or a combination of the following:

The shortness of the season with its attendant increase in overhead costs per performance.

The undesirability of raising ticket prices to a level where they can cover *all* of the rapidly rising costs of performance.

The limited capacity of the hall necessary for a performance of high quality in terms of acoustics and a desired intimacy with the audience.

The necessity of incurring heavy costs for large casts or ensembles, for artists with sufficient reputation to attract patrons, and for qualified technical staff.

The difficulty of anticipating the constantly changing and varied demands of the audience and the unwillingness of the audience, in many instances, to attend performances of new or experimental works.

BOX OFFICE FOR THE DIFFERENT ARTS

Symphony Ticket Sales

As a group, the nation's twenty-five major symphony orchestras presently receive about 52 percent of their total expenses from the sale of tickets, with individual orchestras ranging from 29 percent to 75 percent.

There are a number of reasons our major symphony orchestras do not make their way at the box office. The most pervasive is simply that a symphony concert of top quality is so costly that, using a hall of necessarily limited size, it is not possible to play enough concerts at feasible ticket prices to make box office receipts cover costs.

If prices were scaled at what the traffic could bear, it is possible that a few of the major orchestras could pay all their expenses by the sale of tickets. But in pricing tickets these groups recognize the obligations of nonprofit organizations to try to give access to their performances to the community as a whole. They scale ticket prices accordingly. The price range of the New York Philharmonic is from $1.25 to $7.50; the Boston Symphony Orchestra from $.60 to $7.50; and the Philadelphia Orchestra from $2 to $6.50. Since these orchestras play long seasons with capacity houses at nearly every concert, it seems probable that tickets could be priced higher. But doing so would defeat their purpose as a community cultural resource.

A major symphony orchestra, consisting of from 85 to 106 professional musicians under the leadership of a distinguished conductor, is an expensive organization. The rehearsal requirements, both in time and expense (the musicians are paid for rehearsals), place a limit on the number of concerts that can be given over any period of time. There may be as many as five rehearsals for a week's series of four performances, each rehearsal lasting as long as three hours, and rehearsal requirements become more exacting if the orchestra programs new or difficult works. The major symphony orchestras play in halls ranging in capacity from 1,800 to 5,700 seats, but the satisfactory size is felt to be in the 2,500 to 3,500 range. They perform in communities of varying size, with different income patterns and musical traditions. These factors all play a part in accounting for the fact that subsidy is essential to the financial sustenance of the nation's major orchestras. The same truth holds, often in greater degree, for the nation's other professional symphony orchestras.

The High Cost of Grand Opera

For the nation's handful of major opera companies, the box office presently pays an average of 70 percent of the costs of operation. For individual companies, the box office pays as much as 80 percent in the case of the Goldovsky Opera Theatre and as little as 33 percent for the Santa Fe Opera in New Mexico.

The reasons the box office does not pay the way for opera companies are much the same as those that apply to symphony orchestras. In degree, however, there is one important difference: The major opera companies charge a higher scale of prices for their tickets than orchestras, accounting for the higher average share of the box office contribution to meeting opera's costs.

It is obviously more expensive to present a performance of grand opera in the grand manner than it is to present a symphony concert. Together with a galaxy of international singing stars and leading conductors, the Metropolitan Opera employs a full orchestra, a full chorus, a full ballet, and, as phrased by Anthony A. Bliss, president of the Metropolitan Opera Association, "a repertory of stage productions vaster in size than even the most ornate Broadway musicals." However, with a top of $13 for certain box seats and with a season of approximately two hundred performances in New York and a touring season of about forty-five performances—thirty-three weeks in all—the box office pays 74 percent of total costs. The Staatsoper in Vienna covers only 30 percent of its costs at the box office, La Scala in Milan only 20 percent.

It is conceivable that the Metropolitan Opera could scale its ticket prices to pay all of its costs of operation. The feasibility of such an arrangement would be increased, of course, if the Met were to limit its repertory to tried and true old favorites, which inevitably sell out, avoiding any new or experimental productions. But the Met elects to hold prices below the maximum in order to broaden the availability of its art. Also, by occasionally mounting new and experimental productions, it spends more than commercial calculations might dictate.

There are, of course, less expensive ways of presenting grand opera with artistic success than that followed by the Met and, in large measure, by the Chicago and San Francisco opera companies. The Santa Fe Opera, for example, uses young American singers for its leading roles. In Santa Fe, however, the limited market for grand opera places a relatively low practical limit on what can be charged for tickets. The top ticket price is $6.80 for an outdoor theatre with a maximum seating capacity of 846—accounting for the fact that the box office pays only 33 percent of the total operating expenses. Because it has been playing to capacity audiences, the company plans to increase the number of seats and thereby reduce its deficit.

Chamber and Choral Music

Faced with considerably lower costs, chamber music groups and other small music ensembles seem to have less imposing problems than symphony orchestras and opera companies. But with the taste for such music still relatively undeveloped in the United States, there is also less demand for their services. A few string quartets and small instrumental groups have subsisted on box office receipts, often simply by adjusting downward the compensation for the players. But with the small halls essential to proper performance of this kind of music, chamber music groups of high quality cannot be expected to pay their way at the box office and pay their members adequately at the same time.

Choral music professionally performed is a relatively undeveloped art in the United States, and the demand for it is small. Like any pioneering artistic enterprise, its capacity to generate enough performances is limited. Only Robert Shaw and Roger Wagner have come at all close to establishing "permanent" professional choruses with seasons of sufficient length to provide members with a substantial portion of their incomes.

The Dance

Most major dance groups in the United States fall far short of meeting their expenses from the sale of tickets. Although dancers are generally the lowest paid of the performing artists, company budgets run high. Dance companies usually have a large number of performers, require extensive rehearsal, need music and scenery, and have the continuing expense of mounting new productions. The audience for the dance is still small, and this, too, adds to the difficulties at the box office.

A major segment of the dance world has no institutional support whatsoever. It consists of small companies organized by individual choreographers to give performances whenever money can be gathered together to rent a hall, provide some sort of basic musical accompaniment, and print tickets. This method of doing business almost guarantees box office failure.

The Theatre

On Broadway, in the commercial theatre, box office is counted on to pay the total costs of production and return a profit. If it does not do so or show the potential for doing so, the production closes. But in the nonprofit theatre, if the organization fulfills its community and artistic obligations, the chance of its making its way at the box office is radically reduced, if not eliminated. Implicit in these obligations, for example, are keeping the great classics of the theatre alive and striking out boldly with experimentation in new forms of dramatic writing, acting, and staging. To do this, it is necessary to have a more unified and broadly trained dramatic organization than is needed in the commercial theatre, and the cost of maintaining it, including long-term contracts, tends to mount accordingly.

The nonprofit permanent professional theatres generally take a middle course between the traditional repertory theatre and the continuous presentation of a single play until the audience ceases to come, as is characteristic of the commercial Broadway theatre. These companies are organized on what might be termed a "modified repertory" basis. Most of them do not change their plays for each performance, as in the traditional repertory theatre, but over a season present a number of plays for relatively short periods. This is a financially less exacting as well as a less elaborate method of operation than repertory, with its continuous rotation of actors and settings, but it is more exacting than the Broadway pattern. In the formative years of an organization, even this modified repertory system decreases the possibilities of having the box office pay the costs of operation.

Of the nonprofit permanent professional theatres operating in the 1962–63 season, three—the Arena Stage in Washington, the Tyrone Guthrie Theatre in Minneapolis, and the UCLA Theatre Group in Los Angeles—reported operating surpluses. In 1963–64, only the Tyrone Guthrie Theatre had a surplus. Other theatres reported losses ranging up to about $500,000. With the usual wide variations, their box office accomplishments were shaped by the facts that seasons varied from ten and a half to fifty weeks; the number of seats from 215 to 2,263; ticket prices from zero (free admission) to a top of $6.50; and costs that would ordinarily have appeared on the ledger as operating expenses had been reduced in some cases by foundation grants and other contributions.

There is reason to expect that more of the nonprofit permanent professional theatres, as they become better known and better established in their communities, will be able to make ends meet some years with box office receipts and still fulfill their special artistic obligations. But this is generally too much to expect in their formative period or in periods when they feel the artistic need to mount special projects. Like the other nonprofit performing arts organizations, those of the theatre need financial support beyond what they can obtain at the box office to fulfill properly their artistic mission.

OTHER EARNED INCOME

In addition to the money taken in at the box office, performing arts organizations can, and generally do, earn some additional income through such arrangements as the sale of their services for broadcasting and recording, concessions, and program advertising. But for all except a few this additional income makes a very minor contribution to paying the bills.

A small number of pre-eminent organizations—the Metropolitan Opera and the Boston, New York, and Philadelphia symphony orchestras—add substantially to their total income by broadcasting and recording. The Boston Symphony Orchestra receives approximately 8 percent of its total earned income from record sales and the Philadelphia Orchestra about 12.5 percent. But this income is exceptional. Of the twenty-five major symphony orchestras, only six significantly supplement their box office income by broadcasting or recording.

As more arts organizations obtain halls, a promising way of substantially increasing earned income other than at the box office will be to make use of halls when they would otherwise be idle. In the first two summers of its operation, for instance, Lincoln Center's income was increased by arranging festival series in Philharmonic Hall, which otherwise would have been vacant. The Metropolitan Opera has increased its earned income by renting out the house ($174,000 estimated for 1964–65) when the opera is not in season. A dark house is an expensive house. Booking on off-nights or off-seasons can provide supplementary dollars to reduce operating deficits. This is no perfect solution, however, for many arts organizations do not own their own halls and are simply tenants.

Ideas for increasing supplemental earned income range from increasing regional television and radio broadcasting by arts organizations to serving refreshments during intermissions. In this connection it is notable that theatre-restaurant combinations have been commercially successful and that near New York City a theatre in a shopping center is operating with commercial success.

For nonprofit performing arts organizations, however, there is no prospect that supplemental earned income can be increased to a point where, combined with box office income, it will make them self-sustaining. On the contrary, the gap between earned income and total costs can be expected to widen in the years immediately ahead. If these arts organizations are to perform their cultural role adequately and compensate their artists and managerial staffs properly, they must have financial support beyond what they can earn by their services.

4
Individual Giving to the Performing Arts

The private donor—the individual, the foundation, the corporation—has the major responsibility for insuring the survival and growth of the performing arts organizations. In 1963, private philanthropy for all purposes reached a total of over $10 billion (table 1), or about 2 percent of the national income. This represented an increase of almost $3 billion, or 40 percent, above 1958.

In the dollar aggregate these figures have been rising impressively. However, cultural activities receive a surprisingly small percentage of the total amount of private

Table 1. Sources of Charitable Contributions

	1963		1958	
	%	Amount	%	Amount
Individuals	78.6	$7,875 million	79.2	$5,650 million
Foundations	8.2	819 million	7.1	505 million
Charitable Bequests	7.9	795 million	6.3	450 million
Business Corporations	5.3	536 million	7.4	525 million
Total	100	$10,025 million	100	$7,130 million

Source: American Association of Fund-Raising Counsel, Inc., *Giving USA*, 1959 edition, p. 7, 1964 edition, p. 10, for dollar amounts; Special Studies staff calculation for percentage figures.

Table 2. Beneficiaries of Charitable Contributions

	1963		1958	
	%	Amount	%	Amount
Religion	49	$4,912 million	51	$3,636 million
Education	17	1,704 million	12	856 million
Welfare	15	1,504 million	18	1,283 million
Health	12	1,203 million	14	998 million
Foundations (paid into)	4	401 million	3	214 million
Other (including civic and cultural)	3	301 million	2	143 million
Total	100	$10,025 million	100	$7,130 million

Source: American Association of Fund-Raising Counsel, Inc., *Giving USA*, 1959 edition, p. 8, 1964 edition, p. 10, for percentage figures; Special Studies staff calculation for dollar amounts.

philanthropy. It is estimated that less than 2 percent (about $200 million) goes to cultural programs of all kinds, with the performing arts receiving much less than half that total (table 2).

SHIFTING PATTERNS OF PRIVATE SUPPORT

But there is nothing immutable about the way the charitable dollar is divided up. Although religious giving has been the largest and most stable element in private philanthropy, there have been changes in the relative positions of the other beneficiaries. These changes reflect long-term shifts in the pattern of American philanthropy.

Prior to World War I the main emphasis was on welfare—the Victorian concept of charity. After World War I greater concern for health developed, and a broad program of research in medicine and public health was added to the traditional concern for individual welfare. This combination was dominant in shaping the nature of charitable contributions in the years between the wars.

After World War II the needs of education moved toward the foreground, and the formation in 1952 of the Council for Financial Aid to Education served to emphasize to the business community the rapidly expanding needs of higher education—demands that the launching of Sputnik in 1957 elevated to emergency proportions. Since then, the share of private giving for education has steadily risen, with an offsetting decline in giving for health and welfare.

It is only in the past few years that cultural activities have entered seriously into competition for the philanthropic dollar. But, as noted, they remain the least significant aspect of American philanthropy.

For their proper development in the United States the performing arts obviously must receive far greater private support—from individuals, business corporations, and foundations—than they now receive.

THE INDIVIDUAL

Now, as in the past, it is the individual—not the foundation nor the corporation—who shoulders by far the heaviest share of the responsibility for supporting American nonprofit institutions of all sorts. Individuals contributed 78.6 percent of the $10 billion in 1963. Adding in the 7.9 percent from bequests, we see that individuals were responsible for 86.5 percent of all charitable contributions in the United States in that year.

In the five-year period from 1958 to 1963, individual giving increased 39 percent, foundation giving 62 percent, and bequests 77 percent, while corporate contributions rose only 2 percent, despite the fact that over the five-year period of generally expanding prosperity, corporate income before taxes increased by approximately one-third.

In 1962, the last year for which detailed figures are available, the Internal Revenue Service reports that individual contributions totaling $7.5 billion were listed on 26,451,105 itemized tax returns, out of a total of 62,712,386 filed. The balance of the returns were made on short tax forms, which permit a standard flat deduction (10 percent of adjusted gross income up to a maximum of $1,000) for various expenditures, including contributions. Consequently, if the contributions of those who used the standard flat deduction in making their income tax returns were included, the actual figure for total individual contributions would be substantially over $7.5 billion, but there is no way of estimating the figure.

While individuals make by far the largest total contribution to philanthropy, they use only a small fraction of the 30 percent deduction from their taxable income that the federal government now permits. In 1962, the average of itemized contributions by individuals constituted only 3.5 percent of their adjusted gross income—not much more than a tenth of the income-tax-free deduction permitted (table 3). This is one indication of the very large potential

Table 3. Contribution Rates by Income Classes, 1962
(For Itemized Returns)

Adjusted gross income class (thousands)	Number of returns with itemized deductions	Adjusted gross income (thousands)	Contributions (thousands)	Percent of gross income
Under $2.5	2,201,829	$ 3,819,713	$ 222,846	5.8
$2.5 under $5	6,066,492	23,350,615	978,822	4.2
$5 under $10	12,789,514	91,271,458	2,906,017	3.2
$10 under $15	3,534,448	41,897,526	1,270,296	3.0
$15 under $20	861,833	14,680,525	460,846	3.1
$20 under $25	354,815	7,889,986	251,524	3.2
$25 under $50	497,235	16,648,708	559,544	3.4
$50 under $100	118,098	7,769,576	332,638	4.3
$100 under $150	15,549	1,856,452	112,964	6.1
$150 under $200	4,994	854,715	68,899	8.1
$200 under $500	5,126	1,453,300	153,022	10.5
$500 under $1,000	817	543,938	63,884	11.7
$1,000 and more	355	717,179	134,786	18.8
Total	26,451,105	$212,753,691	$7,516,088	3.5

Source: U.S. Treasury Department, Internal Revenue Service, *Individual Income Tax Returns for 1962, Preliminary*, p. 20, supplemented by unpublished material obtained from the Service; Special Studies staff calculation for percent of gross income going to contributions.

for increase in individual contributions to philanthropic enterprises, including the performing arts.

It was not those in the top income brackets who gave most of the $7.5 billion of itemized individual contributions in 1962. More than 50 percent of it came from those with adjusted gross incomes below $10,000, and those in the lower income brackets gave higher proportions of their incomes than any except those in the very high brackets. Going up the adjusted gross income scale, it was not until those with incomes of $100,000 to $150,000 were reached that the percent of income going for charitable contributions (6.1 percent) was greater than that for those with incomes under $2,500 (5.8 percent).

The figures detailed in table 3 suggest that while there is room in every income range for substantial increase in charitable contributions within the deductible limit, the room for expansion is relatively commodious in the range of income from $5,000 to $50,000. There the percentages of philanthropic contributions are consistently less in proportion to income than they are for those with incomes under $5,000. It is in these income tax brackets also where there is the largest part of the total of individual income.

In the past, wealthier individuals have taken the lead in providing support for the arts, and they still have an important role to play. In spite of the greatly increased tax burden on large incomes, there is still much unused financial capacity for support in the high and middle income brackets.

Patterns of Giving to the Performing Arts

While we cannot say how many people contributed how much money to arts institutions in any one year, we do know that donations over the years have become more numerous, if far smaller, than they were some thirty years ago. The classic example of the patron who year after year paid the annual deficit of the Boston Symphony Orchestra with a single check is a thing of the past.

The Orchestra. There is only the sketchiest information about how or how well nonprofit performing arts organizations explore possibilities for individual contributions, with the exception of symphony orchestras, which, thanks to the American Symphony Orchestra League, have some consolidated records of the support they receive. Of the $49 million the country's orchestras spend, roughly $20 million, or 41 percent, must come from sources other than earned income. Of this $20 million, about $12 million

Table 4. Individual Contributions to Symphony Orchestras, 1963–64

Orchestra	Total Contributions from Individuals	Number of Contributions
Atlanta Symphony	$ 17,826	527
Birmingham Symphony	19,566	667
Boston Symphony	229,111	4,882
Cleveland Orchestra	117,608	1,550
Hartford Symphony	93,000	5,205
Los Angeles Philharmonic	237,305	5,705
Minneapolis Symphony	149,246	1,459
Oakland Symphony	59,359	321
Oklahoma City Symphony	65,160	1,731
Omaha Symphony	4,665	139
Richmond Symphony	33,734	369
Syracuse Symphony	27,643	680

Source: Individual orchestras.

is contributed by individuals and business firms, most of it by the former.

A few samplings (tables 4 and 5) underline how sharply patterns have changed from the day when an individual patron or a small group of patrons wiped out an orchestra's annual deficit. Today over 85 percent of the total number of contributions made to symphony orchestras are in amounts of less than $100. Of the 4,882 contributions made to the Boston Symphony in 1963–64, 4,407 were $100 or less.

Table 5. Distribution of Individual Contributions to Symphony Orchestras, 1963–64

	Number of Contributors		
Size of Contribution	Atlanta (1,011,100)	Minneapolis (1,441,700)	Hartford (689,555)
$1– $99	444	1,004	5,067
$100– $499	78	396	106
$500– $999	4	28	15
$1,000–$4,999	1	27	16
$5,000–$9,999	—	4	—
above $10,000	—	—	1
Total Number of Contributions	527	1,459	5,205
Total Amount of Contributions	$17,826	$149,246	$93,000

Source: Individual orchestras. Metropolitan area population figures are from 1960 census.

The Opera. Most performing arts institutions rely on subscribers as the dependable core of financial support. But some opera companies go beyond voluntary contributions and ask subscribers to take on the added role of underwriting deficits as well as simply buying tickets. Each year, for example, the Metropolitan Opera invites its subscribers to contribute 20 percent over and above the fixed cost of tickets. The San Francisco Opera also makes up part of its operating deficit by assessing those who hold boxes for the Tuesday-Friday subscription series an additional $75 to $150.

Chicago's Lyric Opera uses a guarantor system to help cover its operating costs. In the year ending January 31, 1964, the company raised about $321,000 from guarantors who pledged $1,000 or more. Patrons and sustaining members and contributions from other sources brought total contributions to $597,500.

The Santa Fe Opera receives outstanding support from individual contributors. For its 1964 summer season, well over half—$121,000—of its total contributed income of approximately $210,000 came from individuals. Forty thousand dollars came from out-of-state donors because Santa Fe's determinedly experimental approach attracts this national support. It is the only opera, except the Met, to do so.

The Metropolitan Opera, of course, is regarded as much more than a local institution, and thus draws support from a very wide group of people. But it needs a great deal of money to eliminate its operating deficit at the close of each season—$1.75 million for 1963–64. From 20 to 25 percent of this deficit is made up by the contributions from subscribers; the two supporting organizations, the Metropolitan Opera Guild and the National Council, add another $360,000 annually; and the rest (over $1 million) comes from individual contributions. Rudolf Bing believes that the individuals who up to now have been the principal supporters cannot carry a much heavier load and that new sources of support will have to be found.

The Dance. There are very few permanent dance institutions and, therefore, very few of the peripheral organizations and activities that bolster the orchestras, the operas, and the nonprofit theatres. As a rule there are no ladies guilds running bazaars or fashion shows and no subscription lists to be canvassed. Fund-raising drives usually boil down to one or two interested people asking their friends for money. As a result, such individual support as the dance receives usually comes in quite large amounts.

One characteristic of this tradition is that the interest of the leading ballet patrons does not have the detached quality one often finds in the other arts. They are deeply involved in and committed to the art they support, but this small, gallant band cannot be expected to carry the burden of expansion that is now required in this art.

The Theatre. In the nonprofit professional theatre, individual contributions are solicited much as they are in the other performing arts. Since many of these theatres have been recipients of matching Ford grants, total individual contributions to match them have been substantial. The Mummers Theatre of Oklahoma City reports that 42 percent, or $231,000, was raised within three weeks from individual contributions. The largest individual contribution was $70,000, the smallest $1. Fifty percent of the contributions were under $500, but there were several $50,000 and $25,000 contributions from local leaders. The feeling was that the theatre was good for business and was a valuable community asset.

The commercial theatre, by definition not a field for

charitable contributions but an area for risk capital, has undergone such drastic changes that the average theatre investor may find that in midstream he has shifted from being an investor to being a contributor. In fact, the chances are that this will be his financial fate—only one play in four now succeeds financially.

Why They Give

The tax deduction is a powerful incentive, urging people to translate their charitable inclinations into concrete action. But this does not explain the taxpayer's choice of what he supports. The philanthropic donations of an individual are an expression of his sense of community with others, and the more he identifies with some cause, community, or organization, the greater and more consistent his donations will be. These contributions are also conditioned by his awareness of the importance of the enterprise being supported and its needs. The vigor and consistency with which this awareness is cultivated is a key element in stimulating financial support.

Nonprofit performing arts organizations receive powerful help from federal and state governments through the income tax exemption accorded contributions to them. And the 1964 revision of the federal income tax law increased this help by raising from 20 to 30 percent the deduction from adjusted gross income permitted for contributions to them.

Bequests to nonprofit arts organizations are exempt from the federal estate tax. As table 1 indicates, bequests constitute an imposing source of philanthropic contributions. In 1963, they totaled nearly 50 percent more than contributions made by business firms, and, according to an estimate by the Foundation Library Center, total charitable bequests are increasing by about $50 million each year. Bequests almost always go to organizations in which the donor had an active interest during his lifetime. If arts organizations are to become important beneficiaries of bequests, they must first succeed in enlisting lifetime support from individuals.

What Can Be Done

Of course, a substantial portion of the support for the arts will continue to come from a relatively few large donors. *Nevertheless, the panel stresses the value to arts organizations of broadening the base of their financial support. This can only be accomplished if the organizations are imaginative and effective in developing programs to serve the artistic needs of the community and if the public is made fully aware of the significance of the work being done.*

To attract substantial and sustained support an organization must demonstrate that it has responsibility, continuity, and the promise of some stability. The organization must also have clear concepts of its purpose, its development plans, and why its existence is important to the community. And it must communicate these concepts to the public. It may be possible to raise a certain amount of money simply because the solicitors and donors share a general feeling of responsibility to the community, but continuing support must depend on more than that.

The individual differs from other contributors in that he usually has no coordinated program of giving, and no way to develop one; he gives only in response to specific requests and only after the social usefulness of a philanthropic activity has been clearly established in terms that relate to his needs. To convince large numbers of individuals of the importance of the performing arts, it is obviously necessary to mount broad educational campaigns. The seeking of mass support for the arts is a relatively new phenomenon on the American scene, and the relationship of the arts to society has not been universally established in the same way as the "usefulness" of hospitals, churches, and the social welfare agencies has been established. An appeal for broad support of arts organizations is necessarily a complex matter, involving all the resources of advertising and public relations. Making an appeal of this kind is infinitely more difficult than the traditional one of appealing, on a person-to-person basis, to a community's leading citizens for support.

In addition to increased funds, widely based support will pay other dividends by creating a climate of opinion in which corporate and government leaders are encouraged to raise their contributions, too. Indeed, it is only when there appears to be a communitywide consensus in favor of the arts that business and government are likely to make more than token contributions to them.

The key to broadening the base of support is basically a significant program of community service on the part of the arts organization, accompanied by a skillful and energetically conducted education campaign. Not only will funds be raised but, equally important, a virtually permanent corps of volunteers will be recruited who will form the backbone of future drives, and who will also form the core of the audience for the arts. The value of having a large number of people within the community with a direct personal involvement in the fate of the arts cannot be overstressed. Professional fund raisers estimate that there are more than 50,000,000 volunteer money raisers for philanthropic enterprises in the United States, some 18,000,000 of whom are raising money for churches alone. Arts organizations cannot look forward to commanding such massive forces in the near future, but they should be working hard in this direction.

Here again the analogy to higher education should prove encouraging. Years ago colleges and universities leaned heavily on a few alumni who made large gifts. Now the emphasis is on having many alumni participate—even at a dollar a year. The alumni associations recognize that if they are to increase support from all income levels, giving must become a habit. Once an alumnus subscribes, preferably the first year he gets out of school, the chance is reasonably good that he is going to keep on doing it, and probably increase his contribution as his income rises as well.

Attempts to increase and broaden support for the arts are hampered by a tendency on the part of the sponsors of one performing art to deprecate the importance of other performing arts and to discount the importance of cooperation with other community organizations in money raising. This does not strengthen economic support for the arts, individually or collectively. Arts organizations, for example, rarely incorporate their fund-raising efforts in those of other community organizations. In 1964, of the 472 cities reporting to the United Community Funds and Councils of America, only 31 indicated support for arts projects in their budgets and only 9 for the performing arts.

The united method of fund raising is attractive to donors. Businessmen in particular prefer one overall request for funds to multiple solicitations, and they are much more likely to support the arts when they see the arts organizations practice good budgeting procedures and strict accounting methods under the guidance of independent budget committees representing the community at large.

There have been some promising pioneer developments in the united arts fund-raising campaigns conducted by arts councils in fourteen communities. For example, in 1964 the Saint Paul Council of Arts and Sciences raised $275,000; the Winston-Salem Arts Council $68,000; the Cincinnati United Fine Arts Fund $434,000; and the Dallas Community Arts Fund $728,000.

Financial demands are becoming so great that many arts organizations simply cannot individually mount a campaign large enough to attain their goals. In most instances, councils have been able to raise larger sums of money through the united approach than their constituent arts organizations were able to raise in separate campaigns, and the proportionate share of administrative costs generally is substantially lower for the individual organization. Communitywide solicitations can also help broaden the base of public support. For example, the Dallas Community Arts Fund had 1,120 contributors during 1963, its first year, as compared to the 375 contributors to its member organizations before the Fund was in existence. In 1964, the number of contributors was increased to 5,178.

Organizations, such as labor unions, rarely contribute substantially to united funds—for health, welfare, or the arts—from their treasuries. But experience has shown that individual contributions can be greatly increased if union leadership is convinced of the value of the united fund and includes it in its education programs.

Arts councils that engage in fund raising can also play an important role in encouraging the formation of new organizations, which are frequently needed for the effective development of the performing arts. The Saint

Paul Philharmonic Society was created with the help of the Saint Paul Council of Arts and Sciences, and in five years the Society has established the Saint Paul Chamber Orchestra (composed of twenty-five musicians from the Minneapolis Symphony), the Saint Paul Civic Orchestra for nonprofessional musicians, four youth orchestras, and a summer music camp. These programs are under the supervision of a full-time conductor who was brought to Saint Paul with money from the Arts and Science Fund.

Fund raising by the arts councils, especially in the initial campaigns, may, of course, have some drawbacks. Many donors have a personal identification with a specific organization and may contribute less to the arts in an over-all solicitation campaign, even though it is usually possible for the individual donor to designate his pledge to a specific organization. Also, the compromise inherent in united budgeting procedure may require a period of adjustment of member organizations' allocations. On balance, however, the advantages of united fund raising for the arts promise to outweigh the disadvantages in most communities.

It is important for arts organizations to bear in mind that fund raising differs from community to community, from organization to organization. Some organizations and communities rely primarily on corporate giving or foundation giving; others rely on a few very wealthy donors; and still others rely on individual giving. Probably all of these organizations and all of these communities are going to have to learn how to win support from all types of donors. The alert arts organization will try to adapt ideas borrowed from others that have found a successful pattern deviating from its own and not rely simply on time-honored ways of raising money.

5

Corporate Support for the Performing Arts

The arts can be a major source of strength for the business community. They provide cultural resources increasingly recognized as essential to a suitable environment for business enterprise. Their presence or absence in a community frequently plays a role in the decision of personnel to join or stay with a company. Their availability certainly encourages new firms to locate in a city and helps attract tourists and conventions. They help make the increased leisure with which our greater productivity has rewarded us a boon rather than a dangerous emptiness.

They constitute a growing market and provide expanding avenues for employment. There are, therefore, compelling reasons why, in the interest of his community and, indeed, in his own self-interest, a businessman and his firm should be concerned with the cultural and artistic life of his community.

Yet the typical American corporation has so far shown very little enthusiasm for financial support of the performing arts. Indeed, its contribution to philanthropy of all sorts is surprisingly small.

In applying corporate income tax, which takes about half of net corporate income, the federal government permits deductions of up to 5 percent of this income for contributions to charitable and educational organizations, which are construed to include nonprofit arts organizations. The purpose is to provide an incentive for contributions.

It has been the practice of American corporations in recent years to use only a little over one-fifth of the allowable tax exemption. For example, in 1963, the latest year for which complete figures are available, their contributions totaled $536 million, or 1 percent of their taxable income of $51.3 billion. There remained a total of over $2 billion of business income that would have had the government as an equal partner in giving if it had been contributed to eligible nonprofit organizations. Business corporations are an important potential source of financial support for the arts.

TRENDS IN SUPPORT

Although the amounts remain small, corporations during the past quarter of a century have increased their support of philanthropic activities, and there is some evidence of growing interest in the arts. For instance, during

1962, according to a survey of 465 companies by the National Industrial Conference Board, corporate funds allotted to civic and cultural activities were 5.3 cents of each contribution dollar. This was a substantial increase above the average of 3 cents in 1959. The Conference Board found that companies having their own foundations gave more in the civic and cultural category (5.7 percent) than those without foundations (4.9 percent). Larger companies seem to direct less of their contribution budgets for civic and cultural activities than do smaller. The range was from 4.45 percent for companies with over 10,000 employees to as much as 12.11 percent for those with only 500 to 999 employees.

Recently the Rockefeller Brothers Fund surveyed 100 corporations of varying sizes. It learned that 55 percent gave something to the arts. But about half of these gave less than 1 percent of their total contributions to the arts. In some instances in which large grants had been made, the range was from 3 to 7 percent, and one bank allocated 22 percent.

In a 1963 survey by the American Society of Corporate Secretaries, with 346 companies responding, 48 percent reported their companies contributing from 1 to 9 percent of total contributions to cultural activities. Only 5 percent gave more (one company gave nearly 80 percent of its total in support of cultural projects, another reported 50 percent), while 47 percent of the responding companies replied that they make no contributions whatever to the arts, approximately the same as indicated in the Rockefeller Brothers Fund survey.

In summary, it can be estimated that only slightly over half of all corporations in the United States give anything to the arts. Of the total contributions made by all corporations, only a tiny fraction—at most 3 to 4 percent, or some $16 to $21 million in 1963—goes to the arts.

A LEAD BY ARTS ORGANIZATIONS

If the present trickle of corporate support for the arts is to be expanded, both arts organizations and corporate managements have mutual responsibilities to fulfill. As a practical matter, broad recognition of the importance of the arts by the business community will depend primarily on the initiative of arts organizations. There is a tendency on the part of leaders of arts organizations to assume that anyone who is moderately perceptive will understand the significance of the arts. This is a poor assumption.

It is not even safe, as a matter of fact, for an arts organization to assume that the direct economic contribution of the arts to the business community is fully appreciated. The Stanford Research Institute has calculated that in 1960 the arts market, exclusive of books and expenditures for education, was a $2.5 billion market, with 50,000,000 people involved, and by 1970 may approach $7 billion. By 1970, $4 billion will have been spent on new construction of arts centers in the United States and Canada. But these facts are not fully known or appreciated by business.

The contributions of a thriving cultural life to increasing tourist and convention business, attracting new industry, recruiting personnel—particularly when professional people are being transferred to a new location—also need to be stressed. Corporations find that an important consideration in determining the willingness of executive and scientific personnel to move to a new community is the quality of artistic resources offered.

The arts can also help business in coping constructively with the increased leisure created by the shorter work week, earlier retirements, and greater longevity. Business concerns have an interest in seeing that increased leisure is a source of satisfaction—not boredom and frustration.

There has been a growing appreciation that the success of business enterprise is in part measured by its contribution to a better life in the community. As this sense of corporate citizenship has developed, the emphasis in giving has moved from health and welfare to education. The importance of corporate support of the arts, as a matter of civic responsibility, is just beginning to be recognized by business executives. But much remains to be done to make the arts widely regarded as an appropriate object of corporate support—an acceptance that is important in achieving a firm financial underpinning.

A DEMONSTRATION OF GOOD PLANNING

In requesting corporate support, arts organizations should recognize that although corporations have the pursuit of profit as a common purpose they also have a wide variety of individual attributes. Some are national in scope, some are regional, and many are strictly local. Some make extensive use of intellectual and artistic talent, others make relatively little. The products and services of some go largely to youngsters, the products of others to adults. (The toy company is much more likely to contribute to a youth concert than it is to a concert planned for adults.) As a matter of practical strategy, arts organizations should accept responsibility for relating their requests for corporate support to the "personality" of the corporation from which they seek it.

Arts organizations owe it to themselves and to business to make well-reasoned and well-documented cases for corporate support. The most generous and far-sighted corporation still expects the organization seeking its help to prove that it has competent management and a realistic budget, that it is developing other sources of support, and that it has plans to attain both immediate objectives and long-range goals. Responses received in the Rockefeller Brothers Fund survey underlined the importance of responsible planning and good management.

One way arts organizations can improve their managements and sharpen their objectives is to encourage corporate executives to assist them. Mastering the management of a business corporation is no guarantee that a man can automatically transfer his skill to an arts organization. But, given careful orientation, the business executive can be a great help, and he can be particularly effective in making the case for corporate and community financial support.

CORPORATE RESPONSIBILITY

The corporation has to take the initiative in setting its own priorities in giving. Balances shift according to need and in keeping with the corporate interest and understanding. In 1962, for instance, company gifts to education were for the first time greater than those to health and welfare—41.9 percent as against 40.9. Funds allotted to civic and cultural enterprises, which until a few years ago seldom appeared as a budget item, are more in evidence than ever before.

Clearly, it is impractical to set priorities without knowledge and information. Yet the Rockefeller Brothers

Fund survey showed only 3 out of 100 corporations had studied, directly or through company foundations, the possible role of corporate giving to the arts.

WHAT THEY HAVE DONE

Corporate support of the arts can take a notable diversity of forms. Following are a few impressive illustrations of how realistic support can enrich a community's cultural life.

Contributions for operating expenses—either direct or through united arts funds—are extremely helpful and are the most frequent means of support. The Detroit Symphony Orchestra was revived by gifts totaling $412,400, of which $260,000 was donated by twenty-six corporations, with pledges of continued aid over two additional years. A substantial portion of the $120,000 given to cultural activities by the United States Steel Foundation in 1962 was for operating needs of various orchestras and opera companies. Corporations also contributed 44.2 percent of the $433,858 raised in 1963–64 by the United Fine Arts Fund of Cincinnati for support of the symphony orchestra, the art museum, the Taft Museum, and the summer opera.

As well as support for general operations, there have been significant contributions to community development projects. A group of Connecticut insurance companies donated about $450,000 to the capital development campaign of the Hartford cultural center. Both Lincoln Center and the John F. Kennedy Center for the Performing Arts have received substantial support from the business community. In addition to actual dollars given, corporate executives who are involved in urban renewal and other municipal development projects can assure that adequate facilities for the performing arts are considered in urban planning.

Other valuable support of the arts includes making business facilities available to arts groups, encouraging executives to participate in the cultural life of the community, and giving management advice and assistance to arts organizations.

Some corporations are helping to build audiences for the arts through special employee concerts and subsidized tickets for employees. The Archer-Daniels-Midland Company subsidizes a fixed amount of the purchase price of Minneapolis Symphony tickets, and the employee pays the difference, which varies according to location of seats. The Monsanto Company held a concert by Van Cliburn in 1961 for its St. Louis employees, in addition to making annual contributions to some fourteen arts organizations throughout the country. Republic Steel sponsors a "Republic Night" once or twice a year at the Cleveland Play House and a summer concert of the Cleveland Orchestra. The company buys large quantities of tickets at a discount and resells them to the employees at cost.

Sponsorship of the arts on radio and television is another important way corporations can contribute to audience building. Conspicuous examples include the "Bell Telephone Hour," sponsored by the American Telephone and Telegraph Company, Texaco's sponsorship of radio broadcasts of the Metropolitan Opera, and the Standard Oil Company of New Jersey's success with "The Play of the Week," "The Age of Kings," "The Festival of Performing Arts," and "Esso World Theatre." "Esso Theatre, U.S.A.," featuring performances by permanent professional theatres throughout the country, is the most recent in this series.

Commissioning presentation of special works—often beyond the regular operating budget of an arts organization—can significantly enhance the quality of production provided. An outstanding example in 1963 was the gift to the Metropolitan of a new production of "Aïda" by the American Export and Isbrandtsen Lines. In making this gift, a hardheaded business board reasoned, in the words of its chairman, John M. Will: "Our line carries opera stars and other artists who spend a great part of their lives in travel; furthermore we feel that others in all fields may be induced to travel. We're in close contact with the lands that have produced great art since ancient times—Egypt, Greece, Spain, Italy. It seemed a natural." The enthusiastic response of press and public alike appeared to adequately justify the board's action in terms of prestige and public relations alone.

A unique type of corporate support for the arts is the work of the Recording Industries Music Performance Trust Funds, created as part of the settlement of the American Federation of Musicians strike against the recording industry in 1948. The Funds receive from recording companies a payment of 1 to 1.5 percent of the total dollar volume of record sales at "suggested retail price" levels. The Funds are administered by an independent trustee named by the recording companies. In recent years the Trust Funds have received payments exceeding $5 million a year, which must be expended currently. Since establishment of the Funds in 1949, the money has been used for single-engagement free concerts in all parts of the country. Beginning in 1964, the receipts from new production will be divided in half, one half continuing to be used for free concerts and the other half going directly to the musicians who played the original recordings.

Business support for the arts is important in preserving a healthy balance between private and government support. The arts now receive public assistance, particularly at the local level, and more is anticipated. But strong private support is just as essential to the economic structure of the arts as it is to our system of higher education, which receives massive public aid.

UNUSED TAX EXEMPTION

At present only a handful of firms uses the full 5 percent federal income tax exemption for contributions to philanthropic enterprises. This has prompted the president of a corporation that does utilize the full 5 percent to remark:

> . . . in the case of contributions corporate officials do not take advantage of the allowable gifts the federal government has set up. We are in a world competition for survival, and if we do not meet the requirements of a free society to support education, culture, medicine, welfare, etcetera, we will give the rest of the world one good reason to put us in the category of a second-rate nation. . . . the large corporations in this country have the funds to meet the challenge and our government has given them the green light . . . .

Of major importance to the future of the arts are strenuous efforts to stimulate corporations to utilize more of the 5 percent tax deduction that is allowed for philanthropic contributions. If there is fuller general use of this allowance, the arts are likely to gain a fair share of the increase.

Corporation executives frequently say they fear stockholder objection if they raise the amount of charitable deductions. But firms that have done so have encountered little, if any, objection. Many stockholders, as individuals, are heavily involved in charitable activities and understand that the needs of many community organizations require support from a variety of sources, including corporate.

CORPORATE LEADERSHIP FOR THE ARTS

Chambers of commerce, service organizations, and trade associations can provide leadership, particularly in planning convention programs and through educational projects explaining the economic advantages of a thriving cultural life to the business community. Because convention and banquet programers are constantly looking for speakers on provocative subjects, the arts organizations have an excellent opportunity to present their case before these groups.

Business associations could become a focus for combined civic-corporate promotion of the community's cultural needs. The associations could inform their constituents of the needs of the arts (with the help of representatives of arts organizations), suggest the most fruitful avenues for corporate support, and also undertake specific tasks, such as reminding the national corporations of their responsibilities to the communities in which they have branch offices. This is particularly important now when mergers have often dried up corporate support at the community level because the parent organization does not see its opportunity to serve the community in which its affiliates do business.

Many companies could increase their support for the arts by matching employee gifts to performing arts organizations. About 250 companies now have programs through which they match their employees' contributions to colleges, universities, and sometimes pre-college institutions. This idea began in 1955 with the inauguration of the Corporate Alumnus Program by the General Electric Company. An employee gift-matching program is easily administered and is readily adaptable to support of the arts. So, too, is the arrangement for payroll deduction of contributions to the arts, which Braniff Airways pioneered for the convenience of its Dallas employees.

In some communities, notably Cleveland, corporations have joined in a compact to contribute 1 percent of their pre-tax profits to colleges and universities. This type of cooperation on a widespread basis would go far toward making the present financial distress of higher education largely a matter of unhappy history. The same would, of course, be true for the arts.

An organization patterned on the Council for Financial Aid to Education would be useful in stimulating corporate giving to the arts. This Council, incorporated in 1952 and financed first by foundations and then by business corporations themselves, has a governing board of distinguished business and educational leaders and a small professional staff. A similar council for the arts could encourage increased financial support from all logical sources; improve the climate for voluntary support of the arts; help convince executives that company self-interest is served by support of the arts; provide information about present support and about what arts organizations need; advise on specific aid programs for the arts; and cooperate with any associations, groups, or organizations interested in development and support of the arts.

Leadership in investing in the artistic life of a free society, based on reasoned policy, is the opportunity now afforded the corporation. *Corporate dollars are important dollars, capable of making the difference between life or death for an arts organization. If business corporations have not done so, as most of them have not, the panel urges that they look carefully at the arts and their place in the community. Support for the arts is a part of community responsibility, and a healthy cultural environment is clearly in the self-interest of the business community.*

6
Foundation Support for the Performing Arts

The innovative role of the charitable foundation in American society has been long and distinguished. However, with a few exceptions, foundations have not yet come to recognize the arts as a field as important as education, scientific research, and welfare, which until recently have claimed their primary attention. Foundations, large and small, national and local, could play a significantly larger role in the development of the arts than they have in the past.

SEEKING FOUNDATION SUPPORT

Arts organizations have not adequately made their case for foundation support and, in comparison with other claimants on foundation resources, suffer all too often from poor management and inadequate planning.

Even foundations that might be inclined to support the performing arts complain that arts organizations characteristically ignore the financial facts of life, are frequently careless in their managerial procedures, and expect to be supported without providing a plausible projection of future expenditures. Unquestionably, many groups should make a greater effort to put their houses in order before seeking outside support. Lack of funds is often the reason given for failure to follow good management procedures, but this is hardly a valid argument.

The transient or disorganized pattern of so many arts organizations has contributed to the foundation preference for projects with established institutions or programs in universities where competent administrative personnel and continuity increase the prospects for constructive use of a grant. It is to be noted in this regard that foundations —as well as arts organizations—frequently overlook the important contribution foundation executives can make in giving guidance in organization and management.

Too often, "The Foundation" is thought of as a bottomless reserve of funds, the cure for all financial ills. Nothing could be further from the truth. Foundation funds are far from limitless, and those now available for the performing arts represent only a tiny fraction of the whole. For arts organizations to turn to foundations, large or small, in hopes that their needs will be swiftly satisfied, is almost certain to lead to disappointment.

Arts organizations, in addition to realizing that available funds are limited, would also be well advised to recognize the differences among foundations. In many cases even cursory inquiry would reveal the futility of spending time and effort on appeals to foundations with programs that clearly exclude the arts or ones that have made amply clear the particular limits of their interest in the arts. An arts organization should only approach those foundations it finds reason to believe will seriously consider its request.

For the purpose of distinguishing foundation roles, a rough measure of size and focus of interest is adequate. There are some fifteen thousand grantmaking foundations in the United States. Of these, 176 foundations have assets of $10 million or more and possess more than 76 percent of total foundation assets in the country. The top 10 have about 40 percent. The large foundation usually has an active board of trustees and at least one full-time professional employee to develop its program. The small foundation is most often guided by the goals of one individual and has no full-time professional staff, and many are limited by their charter to specific fields of endeavor.

While size does not invariably dictate program, the arts organization should understand that it is generally true that the purposes of almost every grant made by a large foundation are at least partially national in scope, while the small foundation usually concentrates on its own geographic area or on a special purpose. There is no likelihood, for example, that a large national foundation would respond favorably to requests for ongoing support of strictly local efforts, unless there is some specific interest in the locality or a significant pilot aspect to the project.

The need to distinguish between the roles of the

national and local foundation is particularly important in requesting contributions for general operating expenses. The local foundation is, in many cases, taking the place of the individual donor. With the traditional patrons increasingly making charitable contributions through their own foundations, it is reasonable to expect these foundations to provide general support funds. Many local foundations *are* doing just this.

With respect to the time period of grants, the large national foundations are generally opposed to long-term commitments. It is felt that funds are more effective if they are given over a limited period, as seed money, with the anticipation that the organization will be able to develop other sources of support if the project is successful. Foundations may begin to modify this policy as the long-term needs of arts organizations increase and are more widely understood. But at present, arts organizations are bound to be rebuffed if they base their appeals to large national foundations on the expectation of indefinitely continuing help.

Whether they are approaching a national or local foundation, arts organizations must state their case coherently and fully. This is not a matter of public relations technique but of making a reasonable attempt to project future programs and needs and demonstrating a conscientious effort to develop other sources of funds. In many communities the argument for support must begin at the most basic level. Arts leaders must be prepared to discuss the nature of the arts, why they are important, and why foundation support of this still-minority interest is justified. They must work hard because the case for the arts is less readily evident than that of education or medicine.

The case must be well thought through and be understood by everyone who expects to make headway with the foundations or any other potential source of support.

FOUNDATION GIVING

Total foundation giving in 1963 amounted to $819 million, only 8.2 percent of all philanthropy. Current foundation support for the performing arts is minuscule, although in 1963 the figure rose sharply because of the $20.2 million contributed to Lincoln Center for the Performing Arts, the Houston Endowment grant of $6 million for a performing arts center, and the Ford Foundation grants of $6 million to nonprofit permanent theatres. Aside from these contributions, foundations as a whole are still allocating a very small percentage of their spendable funds —an estimated 1 to 2 percent—to the performing arts.

Nonetheless, on the assumption that the Ford Foundation will continue its program on at least its present level, and on the evidence of some general increase in foundation concern with the performing arts, it can be estimated that some $20 to $30 million will have been directed to this area during 1964. This may amount to between 3 and 4 percent of the total foundation dollar.

The Local and the Special Purpose Foundations

While the local foundation has the same basic goals as the large national one—to determine the critical areas of public concern and take a sustained approach in dealing with them—its operating patterns are different because its financial capacity usually is smaller, although a few are of substantial size, and its defined community is local or special in nature. The local foundation can make its greatest contribution by fostering the stability of established organizations and by encouraging the development of new cultural resources and audiences in the community.

Perhaps more important than any innovative role is the steady general support of performing arts organizations at the community level that the local foundation is in a unique position to give. Individual contributions vary from one year to the next; special projects attracting support from the large national foundations come and go; box office receipts rise and fall. But the need for constant stable assistance that can be depended on year in and year out remains. Too many local foundations have yet to recognize this need for recurring grants. *The panel believes the role of the local foundation in providing continuing support cannot be overestimated. Indeed, it may turn out to be as important as any single factor in the development of the arts.*

Annual grants that can be counted on are extremely important. In 1963, for example, 26 percent of the contributions to general operating expenses for the Spring Opera of San Francisco came from local foundations, several grants being as small as $25 and $50, the largest $5,000. Endowing an arts organization is, of course, another effective way of insuring a steady source of funds. The Howard Heinz Endowment and the Mellon trusts were the major contributors in establishing an endowment of more than $5 million for the Pittsburgh Symphony Orchestra in 1963. As recognized in this instance, it is essential that endowment funds be thought of as merely supplemental to annual financial support from the community at large.

While few of the small local foundations have professional staffs, the person most responsible for decisions is usually aware of the needs of the community, or if not, can find someone who is. Therefore, the local foundation is in a position to encourage the development of new cultural resources. Does the city really need an arts center? Could an opera company be created if given a strong push? Would a community arts council encourage the growth of cultural resources? These are all questions that need to be asked and if answered affirmatively require money. The Hill Family Foundation, for example, local in character but large in size, has been one of the most active in supporting the development of new arts resources in its community. Its three-year grant of $64,000 launched the Saint Paul Council of Arts and Sciences; its $25,000 to the Saint Paul Civic Opera Association enabled the engagement of a full-time director; its $50,000 assisted the Tyrone Guthrie Theatre in defraying administrative expenses before it opened.

Audience education, of crucial importance for increasing public support for all arts organizations and for providing another element of stability, is also a likely area for the local foundation. Audiences for tomorrow must be developed today, and foundation programs toward this end can be particularly useful, especially if they are worked out in cooperation with other groups. The Kulas Foundation, for example, gives the Cleveland Orchestra $18,000 annually toward its series of children's concerts, and it also subsidizes reduced-rate tickets for various musical events for students and faculty at eleven colleges and other institutions. The Hartford Foundation for Public Giving provides a good example of how a foundation can simultaneously aid audience education and establish a cooperative relationship with local government. Beginning in 1959, it has made grants to the Connecticut Opera Association ($18,000 for the two-year period of 1964–65) to enable students, teachers, and hospital and social agency employees to buy reduced-rate tickets. This encouraged the public schools to support the program by buying blocs of tickets in advance of the performances. The Eugene and Agnes E. Meyer Foundation in Washington, D.C., has made grants to the Washington Opera Society to initiate a series of professional opera presentations in the schools.

The special purpose foundations should be mentioned here. Some of them are of substantial size and have professional staffs. Their community is not defined by geographic lines but by focus of interest. For example, the Elizabeth Sprague Coolidge Foundation has practically singlehandedly stimulated greater interest in chamber music. The Fromm Music Foundation encourages contemporary composers by providing the funds for performance as well as the fee for the composition. The Koussevitzky Music Foundation, too, has given great assistance to contemporary music. The Martha Baird Rockefeller Fund for Music programs are aimed at a variety of activities to enhance the musical arts in the United States, including grants-in-aid to young artists and scholars to assist them in developing professional careers.

Some of the special purpose foundations serve as almost the sole support for certain arts organizations. This kind of arrangement is feasible as long as the relationship between both parties remains amicable. But real difficulties can arise—even the abrupt demise of an organization—when a sole source of support and the recipient come to a parting of the ways without alternative sources having been developed.

The Large National Foundations

The panel believes the large national foundation can make its greatest contribution to the arts in planning and innovation. It has a special capacity to determine the most critical areas of national concern and to devise effective means of solving basic problems. Available funds could not, of course, satisfy the total financial needs of the arts, even if foundations were inclined to try, but they are sufficient to undertake experimental programs and demonstration projects and to assist in the development of nationwide and regional programs and organizations. Projects designed to encourage and guide new sources of support are of particular value.

Demonstration Projects and Experimental Programs. In undertaking experimental projects, the large national foundation can exercise considerable leverage with relatively small amounts of funds. Through its grants, it has the power to validate the appeals of an organization or a project for community support. A striking example of this has been the effect of the Ford Foundation's program of support to professional resident theatres. According to Jules Irving, director of the Actor's Workshop in San Francisco, the Ford program has been helpful in creating a more positive reception to the theatre's requests for funds from other sources. Potential contributors had previously tended to view the theatre as a strictly commercial operation.

When foundations make grants on a matching basis, they serve to encourage other sources of patronage, assuring a broader base of community support. The Oklahoma City Mummers Theatre fund-raising drive to match the Ford grant already mentioned provides an extraordinary example. The Theatre raised a total of $750,000 in three weeks. The Alley Theatre in Houston raised $1.1 million to qualify for a Ford Foundation grant of $2.1 million for construction of a new building and assistance in meeting operating expenses for ten years. The matching grant does carry with it a certain danger of monopoly. It is the responsibility of foundation and community alike to use their resources in ways that will not adversely affect other worthwhile local ventures by causing delay or cancellation, but this is a matter of balance and judgment in each situation for which no formula can be established.

In the arts there are serious gaps between the new creative talent and the seasoned writer, between the inexperienced performer and the trouper, between the cultural capital of the nation and the rest of the country. Examples serve to illustrate how national foundations can help bridge these gaps.

In the development of a playwright's technique, performance on a stage is essential, yet funds for staging a new play by an unknown writer are extremely difficult to obtain. The Ford Foundation announced in October 1964 the third in a series of programs to assist the dramatic writer. A sum of $325,000 will be available over a three-year period to provide opportunities for playwrights to work with nonprofit professional companies and to encourage production of new scripts. A grant of $225,000 was also made to the American Place Theatre, which was founded in 1963 to encourage writers of talent—poets, novelists, historians—to write for the theatre. Its program includes full professional production of completed works for a membership audience.

The growing pains felt by a young actor in moving from amateur to professional theatre are another problem, and fellowships for apprentice training are one answer. In opera, the Avalon Foundation has made grants to the Santa Fe Opera in support of an apprenticeship program under which young singers are given an opportunity to sing in the chorus and play small roles. The National Music League takes another approach. It is a nonprofit concert management organization, supported in part by foundation funds, which gives young artists who have not yet achieved recognition an opportunity to gain concert experience by obtaining engagements for them.

If the theatre, in particular, is really to develop on a wide geographic basis, funds are needed to encourage actors, designers, and technicians to explore the theatre world outside New York and to participate in it. Several Ford programs have experimented in this direction.

The performing arts also need support in exploring new developments. Contemporary music, for example, has received some assistance from foundations but needs more. In 1953, the Rockefeller Foundation made a grant of $400,-000 to the Louisville Orchestra for a ten-year project for commissioning, performance, and recording of new works. The Foundation announced in the summer of 1964 a program of grants that now enables seven symphony orchestras to extend their seasons with a series of well-rehearsed first performances of symphonic works by American composers. These extra concerts will be undertaken in cooperation with nearby universities, and the orchestras will also participate in workshops for outstanding music students.

In another sphere, a review is required of the entire system of publishing and distributing new music. As economic patterns have changed, this can no longer be done adequately by publishers, commercial or nonprofit, without some form of outside assistance.

National and Regional Programs and Organizations. In addition to experimental and demonstration projects, the large national foundations could have a significant impact on the arts by helping establish national and regional programs and organizations. Frequently the funds needed for these purposes are difficult to raise from a single community or donor because the activity is not confined to one locality.

Regional organizations are particularly needed in some of the arts. In opera, for example, outstanding national and regional touring companies hold the most promise, at least until sufficient audiences develop for more localized efforts. National foundation support can be especially effective in establishing and strengthening such groups.

Another illustration points up the importance of being able to concentrate funds on a specific target through a national program. Many observers believe that drastic action is needed to save dance in this country. There have been many critics of the Ford Foundation grant of $7,756,000 announced in 1963 because it was directed primarily to traditional ballet. But the spreading of such funds among all claimants of stature could scarcely have made a comparable impact on the future of dance in America. The Ford grant has acted as a challenge to those who represent different approaches to dance and already new funds from different sources have been forthcoming to support other efforts.

Not only are more arts organizations needed but the management of those in existence badly needs improvement. The surface has just been scratched by existing apprenticeship programs. There is an opportunity for the large national foundations to play a more important role in solving this problem than they have so far. Is there need, for example, for a school of arts administration? What are the qualifications of a good administrator in this complex field?

Better means of collecting and disseminating information could be an important aid to good administration in the arts. Arts organizations themselves, with their own financial burdens, are not likely to concentrate sufficient funds or attention on the establishment of a central source of information. Initiative must come from the outside. Foundation funds have created and are supporting such projects as the Foundation Library Center, which serves a similar need in a comparatively new field.

The lack of specific research on the arts is remarkable considering the magnitude of the problems, and it is a lack the large foundations could help correct. Except for the congressional hearings in 1961 and 1962 on economic conditions in the performing arts, there has been virtually no systematic effort to review the support and development of the performing arts in this country. The economic study now underway by the Twentieth Century Fund will be a particularly significant contribution and should highlight the need for continuing research.

We do not really know much, for example, about the long-term effect of educational projects to develop appreciation and understanding of the arts. Without some appraisal, soundly based educational programs can hardly be developed with any confidence. We also need to know more about the fixed and varying elements of cost in a well-conceived arts program, and useful analyses are needed in every area of production expense: buildings, scenery, lighting, promotion, extension of seasons, salaries.

FLEXIBILITY IN APPROACH TO THE PERFORMING ARTS

Flexibility in foundation giving is essential. Many foundations claim that support for the performing arts is outside the scope of their normal activities. Charter restrictions are sometimes cited as the reason for this limitation on activity, but foundation charters are usually drawn so the board or the donors have ample latitude to change direction if they choose. The trouble usually is that other fields have higher priorities and that not much is known about the arts and their specific needs. Growing public interest is beginning to have its effect in lessening both these restraints, but many foundations remain insulated from the arts and their problems.

An important requirement is the acceptance of risk. It is unrealistic for foundations or any other patrons to expect that any project in the arts will be a guaranteed success. Because decisions on arts applications involve judgments of quality in an area where there are few absolute standards, there is perhaps greater uncertainty about making grants than in the traditional areas of foundation support. But the ever-present possibility of failure should not obscure the need for experimentation.

The arts and artists must be accepted on their own terms, not an unorthodox requirement when we consider the amount of freedom accorded scientists and educators by those who support them. Acceptance of this fact of artistic life is, however, difficult for many people. Artists are frequently inarticulate in explaining their plans and procedures. They are also sometimes rather hostile to the uninitiated outsider, however good his intentions, however deep his concern. Thus patience and acceptance of occasionally difficult personal relations are a necessity in supporting the arts. Sometimes they are almost as important as the willingness to take risks on difficult projects and to stay with them through periods of disappointment and lack of apparent progress.

Related to this problem is the traditional foundation inclination to support research and training rather than performance, regardless of the field. National foundation grants in health and welfare are usually not to hospitals or to service organizations for the blind, the mentally ill, or the disabled; in education, grants are generally not provided for the continuing needs of schools and universities. Even bricks-and-mortar grants are often justified on the ground that they provide needed facilities for training and research. But the very essence of the performing arts requires that they be viewed in another framework. A play, a piece of music, or the outline of a ballet has only a partial existence on paper. Performance before a live audience is itself part of the process of realizing a work of art. This unique characteristic of the performing arts is not widely understood as yet by philanthropic sources.

THE CONTINUING CHALLENGE

The performing arts offer foundations a particularly good opportunity to exercise the initiative and imagination that have so often characterized their contribution to American life. In a field the importance of which has not yet been totally recognized by people generally, but which is nevertheless important to a well-balanced society, foundations have the opportunity to lead in the nourishment and stabilization of the performing arts organizations.

They can accomplish this at two levels. The local foundation is in a unique position to provide the steady operating support that so many arts organizations need. At the national level, the large foundation has the opportunity to encourage experimental projects of all sorts. These may include, certainly, new productions and new production styles, but they may also include essential experimentation in new methods of organizing the business side of the arts or in establishing national and regional combinations of arts organizations, leading to greater efficiency of operation and to the creation of new and larger audiences. In short, both the well-publicized national foundations and the less well-known, but no less vital, local foundations have significant roles to play.

This does not mean foundations should assume the total burden of the arts organizations' almost inevitable deficit. This would be as unhealthy as it would be impracticable. But in applying thought, time, and moderate funds toward the problems and needs of arts organizations, the foundation can do what no other institution has the means and knowledge to do.

The panel urges foundations to increase their interest in the arts and in so doing to recognize the necessarily speculative element in the development of the performing arts and give particular encouragement to the bold and the venturesome—an encouragement they are especially equipped to provide.

7
Government and the Arts

Through the centuries, the governments of most great states and cities have participated in promoting the arts and enriching the lives of their citizens. It has been generally recognized that societies are ultimately judged by the quality of their cultural life; that the worlds of the artist, the dramatist, and the poet outlive more transient victories and defeats. It his been known, too, that the happiness of the citizens is related to the variety and depth of the cultural experiences open to them.

Early American statesmen were aware that the arts could not be neglected if the young Republic was to play its full role in the world. This conviction was particularly obvious in city planning and public architecture. Elsewhere, it is true, the Puritan tradition worked from the beginning against the more worldly appreciation of men like Washington, Jefferson, and Adams. Later the preoccupation of the American people with the westward march and with the development of material wealth made public cultivation of the arts seem a remote concern.

Yet as Americans were turning their attention to pursuits that seemed more pressing, other nations were continuing to develop patterns of support for the performing arts that have come to be the envy of many who practice those arts here. Sweden, France, Italy, and Austria, where the most important cultural organizations have long been subsidized by the central government; Germany, where the states (*Länder*) are largely responsible for these institutions; Great Britain, where in the last twenty years tradition has been reversed and the nation, through the British Arts Council, has begun giving support to the key cultural institutions; Canada, where less than ten years ago a council was established to administer a University Capital Grants Fund and an Endowment Fund that includes the arts—all these have lately been much on the minds of Americans concerned with the arts. They observe in other countries flourishing institutions in which artistic freedom, far from being threatened by the activity of the state, is actually enhanced, and they wonder if we should not attempt to emulate at least some aspects of the European and Canadian patterns here.

The experience abroad is not entirely applicable to the situation in the United States. The differences are in large part occasioned by our attitude toward government and our strong tradition of voluntary association to support community activities. Nonetheless, the lessons of history and the examples of virtually all the other great nations cannot be ignored. We have reached a point in our history where we must come to grips with the question of the role of government in our cultural life. Indeed, from Theodore Roosevelt through Lyndon B. Johnson there have been intermittent but growing efforts to affirm and define public responsibility in the arts. Increasingly, the question has been not whether government should act but how it should act and at what level and by what principles it should shape its policy.

The rule that should determine the government's relation to the arts is basically the same as that which shapes its role generally. It has never been stated better than it was by Abraham Lincoln: "The legitimate object of government is to do for a community of people whatever they need to have done, but cannot do at all, or cannot so well do, for themselves, in their separate and individual capacities. In all the people can individually do as well for themselves, government ought not to interfere."

In spite of the great increase of interest and participation in the arts, the studies of this panel confirm the fact that the professional performing arts are encountering increasing financial difficulties. Private sources alone do not produce the financial support required, and in most communities cultural opportunities remain inadequate or nonexistent. More and more voices propose that the performing arts turn to government for aid. They say very simply that the arts should be made far more widely available to the many than it is possible to make them by private support alone. It is therefore necessary to explore the present and potential roles of governments in supporting the arts.

The panel believes no form of government aid to the arts should vitiate private initiative, reduce private responsibility for direction, or hamper complete artistic freedom. These must remain the prerogative of the citizens who direct performing arts institutions and of the artists. The problem is to determine what kinds of aid government can provide and what techniques it can use in providing them without violating the principles just enunciated.

No rigid pattern of aid can be laid down. Needs vary from community to community, from region to region. Some aims are best accomplished by local governments, others by state governments, still others by the federal government. In general, however, the local government is best suited for assuring that adequate opportunities are available for its citizens to enjoy the arts. It also has a heavy responsibility in seeing that appreciation for the arts is developed in the school system. State governments are best suited to sponsor touring activities and to promote cooperation between arts organizations within the state. They, too, are probably in the best position to promote regional cooperation between the arts organizations of several states. As to the federal government, it has a vital function in setting a national tone of interest in and concern with the arts. It, too, can be an important force in fostering cooperation between organizations and between government agencies concerned with the arts, and it is uniquely placed to study our cultural growth in broad, long-term perspective.

THE LOCAL ROLE—MUNICIPAL AND COUNTY

The cities have traditionally been the home of the arts. Through the ages, as men freed themselves from the necessity of devoting all their time and labor to wresting a living from the soil, they gathered in communities where the pleasures of life could be cultivated—where philosophy, politics, and the arts could find expression. The great cities of Europe became in themselves works of art, and those who ruled them were at pains to see that opportunities for cultural enjoyment existed on a wide scale.

The United States has lived most of its history under the domination of ideas that tend to equate virtue with life on the land and corruption and decadence with urban existence. This is one reason we have allowed our cities to grow in ugliness, largely devoid of cultural attractions. Twentieth-century America is only now facing the fact that it is inescapably an urban civilization and that the quality of its life must ultimately depend upon what men make of their metropolitan centers. American cities are now being rebuilt on a hitherto unimagined scale. It is important that the cultural life of these cities be re-examined and that it be asked how, in the course of this rebuilding process, they may provide citizens with greater opportunities for aesthetic enjoyment.

City and county governments have already developed a variety of channels for economic aid to the arts. The vigor and imagination with which these channels are used, however, vary greatly from one place to another, and from one art to another. Some cities provide sizable financial support for the arts. Others spend little or nothing, and a few impose onerous tax burdens.

Local support for the performing arts is a recent and limited development, particularly in comparison to assistance for the visual arts. There are instances of city contributions to symphony orchestras dating back to the years before World War II, but in most cases support has come within the past ten years. Municipal or county support for opera is found in a few cities, and support for drama and dance in fewer still. In the aggregate, however, local government aid for the arts is growing at a significant rate.

The panel believes every local government should have as an accepted goal the strengthening of local arts organizations and the broadening of their service to the community. For example, by insuring adequate facilities for performance; providing funds for operating costs; supplying supporting services; purchasing the services of the arts for schools and the community; exempting arts organizations from taxes and license fees; helping mobilize community support for the arts.

Adequate Facilities Are Necessary

The absence of suitable facilities is often a definite handicap to arts organizations, and rental, purchase, or construction may be beyond the resources of a single institution. Here there is every reason for local government to participate with private and other government agencies in providing needed facilities. As Theodore R. McKeldin, former Governor of Maryland and now Mayor of Baltimore, states: "We have learned the hard way that to permit the creation of flimsy, jerry-built structures means creating slums that will be breeding places of poverty, disease, and crime. But we have been much slower to realize that the cultural atmosphere of a city is as important as its physical element. The question, therefore, that should concern every American who shares the responsibility for building an American city is only secondarily a matter of extension of its area and population, or even of its economic resources. If it is to be truly great, these things must yield priority to the things that stimulate the spiritual and intellectual growth of its people."

City participation may take the form of permitting the use of city-owned facilities either without charge or at low rentals. There are two rental scales for use of the new Ford Auditorium in Detroit, with commercial organizations paying a higher rent. San Francisco's War Memorial Auditorium is made available for performances by arts organizations at a flat rate for the house, whereas other users pay the flat rate plus a percentage of gross. The St. Louis Symphony Orchestra is allowed to use the city-owned Kiel Auditorium rent-free, paying only the cost of services. These few examples are typical of cities throughout the country.

A striking example of city, state, and private cooperation to preserve an existing facility for the arts was the successful effort to preserve New York's Carnegie Hall. After private owners had announced plans for demolition of the historic building, a committee of citizens persuaded the mayor and governor that the hall should be saved. A special bill was passed by the state legislature enabling the city to buy Carnegie Hall in 1960 for $5 million. It was then leased at an annual rental to a nonprofit, quasi-public body to operate.

City and county assistance are being directed in ever-increasing amounts to the provision of new facilities, particularly cultural centers. In Los Angeles, more than one-third the cost of the $33.5 million Music Center, containing an auditorium and two theatres, is coming from revenue bonds backed by the county, the balance from private contributions.

In some cases the name "cultural center" is attached to what is really a convention center and all-purpose civic hall. Even in these cases it is important to do as much as possible to see that the structure, despite its many purposes, is well adapted to effective use by arts organizations. School halls adequate for performance also can be built at little or no additional cost if planning and forethought are used.

If an *authentic* arts center is projected, great care should be taken with the design and arrangement of physical facilities. Of equal importance is the attention devoted to planning the artistic program for which the facilities will be used, including the maintenance of the performing arts organizations that will occupy the buildings. Without such planning the center will turn out to be a hollow monument to good intentions.

Direct Grants for Operations

Many local governments have for years been making highly beneficial direct contributions to the performing arts with no evidence of political interference. Some examples:

Assistance in covering general operating costs was given by the city of San Francisco in fiscal year 1963–64 to the opera ($80,000), to the symphony orchestra ($80,000), to the ballet company ($30,000), and to the Museum of Art ($40,000), and smaller amounts totaling $45,000 were given to several other professional groups. These funds derive from a 3 percent tax on hotel room occupancy (yielding approximately $1 million a year) that is earmarked for "a publicity and advertising fund" to attract tourist and convention business to the city.

Elsewhere, Salt Lake City appropriates $5,000 per year for the Utah Symphony Orchestra, and New York

City has partially subsidized the New York Shakespeare Festival for the past three years, the current grant totaling $320,000. In Philadelphia, for some years, the city has been contributing $75,000 annually toward the outdoor symphonic concerts in Robin Hood Dell and $25,000 a year each toward the operating costs of two local opera-producing organizations. The city of Baltimore makes an annual grant of $80,000 to the Baltimore Symphony Orchestra. Los Angeles County gives more than $400,000 a year in grants to music organizations, principally for general operating costs.

Many cities earmark aid for specific purposes. In 1964–65, for example, Los Angeles made a sizable ($70,000) contribution from the General City Purposes Fund for publicity and advertising expenses of the Hollywood Bowl Association, the Los Angeles Philharmonic, and some smaller symphonies. The $25,000 given by Oakland, California, to the symphony in 1963–64 was also for advertising and promotion. For the same year, New York City appropriated $125,846 for the Brooklyn Academy of Music, of which about $110,000 was used for salaries of office and maintenance personnel, and the remainder went for supplies, electricity, and telephone costs. Of Buffalo's $50,000 annual appropriation for its Philharmonic, $20,000 was for school concerts and $30,000 for operating expenses, a sum that exactly covered the rent for the city-owned auditorium. Bands established in the late nineteenth and early twentieth century and supported by cities to give free concerts and to perform in parades and other public celebrations continue to receive city support in many communities. There is frequently a combination of support from local civic groups and from the Recording Industries Music Performance Trust Funds.

Supporting Services of Many Kinds

In discussing city support for the performing arts, William B. Hartsfield, Mayor of Atlanta from 1937 to 1961, has observed that outright grants are not the only way a city can help its arts organizations. There are many means by which a city can give assistance that do not require special appropriations. These supporting services can include advertising and promotion, various forms of centralized administrative services, and custodial and maintenance services. The Buffalo Philharmonic Orchestra receives free city office space, including maintenance. Berkeley, California, pays printing costs for the Young People's Symphony. In Atlanta, the city assists the production of summer light opera performances in the park not only through a direct grant of $15,000 but by allowing free use of the amphitheatre, by paying the electric bills, by giving the company the right to operate food and drink concessions, and by providing free parking facilities that are maintained and operated by the city.

Art for the Schools and the Community

The purchase of arts organization services—for public and school performances—probably represents the most customary local government involvement in the arts.

The sale of arts services can have an important by-product: It can enable an arts organization to extend its season and thus provide more employment for its artists. But if the sale of services is to strengthen arts organizations, it is necessary for them to be certain that the purchase price includes the full cost of the services rendered, including overhead. Arts organizations have been careless about this and have sold their services below the true cost, as have colleges and universities in making contracts with the government for research—to their financial sorrow. Arts organizations should be sure they get full payment for services rendered.

Surveys indicate that only a minority of school systems have money specifically provided for the purchase of professional performances for their pupils or for special training in the performing arts. *The panel believes that local governments have a direct responsibility for seeing that study, appreciation, and training in all the arts is an accepted part of the curriculums of their school systems. In the longer view, this panel believes that the provision for adequate education in the performing arts may prove the most effective way by which local governments can promote the well-being of the arts.*

In discharging this responsibility, local governments should expose students to professional performances, either by distribution of free or low-cost tickets or through special presentations within the schools. These performances should not be just warmed-over adult programs but specially designed for children.

Appropriate Tax and Licensing Policies

Where it is legally possible, the earmarking of a portion of the general revenues or the imposition of a special levy for support of the arts can impart real stability and durability to arts organizations. In St. Louis, for example, municipal taxes go to the art museum at a fixed rate of $.04 on $100 of the asessed value of real estate and personal property.

With the exception of some taxes, the burdens imposed

upon performing arts organizations by local governments are relatively few and slight. Licenses for performances and the operation of arts organizations are required by a few cities, and the money collected is almost always absorbed in general funds rather than routed to benefit those paying the license fees. The performing arts would be helped a bit either by being relieved of the licensing requirements or being made direct beneficiaries of the money collected. The arts should also be relieved of the admissions tax imposed by some cities, however light that tax might be.

Another burden, anything but light, is that imposed by those cities that refuse to give nonprofit arts organizations exemption from local taxes on the ground that they are not covered, or not construed to be covered, by laws and regulations pertaining to religious, charitable, and educational institutions. At present the Tyrone Guthrie Theatre, operated as a nonprofit organization, is fighting through the courts what could be a life-and-death battle with Minneapolis authorities who refuse to grant exemption from real estate taxes, which, if levied, would amount to about $75,000 a year. Where necessary, local tax laws should be amended to give nonprofit arts organizations treatment equal to institutions of education and social welfare. This is a basic form of aid to the arts to which localities cannot afford to be indifferent. The very least a city can do for its arts organizations is not place obstacles in the way of their development. The short-term gain accruing to a city from taxes cannot possibly offset the loss its citizens (and perhaps those businesses that are dependent on tourist and convention trade) will feel if the arts organization disappears.

Leadership in Mobilizing Community Effort

Local governments can exercise important leadership in stimulating and mobilizing community support of the performing arts. The mayor of one large city has observed that in many cases a city or municipal organization must "sell" the arts not only to the general citizenry but also to many of the foremost community leaders, a task that frequently involves tactics not so very different from those used to amass support for a sewer loan. The mayor of another large city, Detroit, exercised the authority of his office by increasing the appropriation for school and public concerts (from $50,000 to $57,000 a year), just enough to provide additional funds to break a deadlock in union contract negotiations that had threatened the Detroit Symphony's 1963–64 season.

No elaborate mechanism is needed to provide leadership and to administer the arts policies of a local government. But experience indicates that an effective job requires, in many instances, an imaginative, energetic, and competent individual attached to the mayor's or city manager's office as a cultural officer and given the help of a small staff.

In an increasing number of cities arts councils are playing an important role in coordinating various individual arts organizations and practices. Some of these are private bodies, a few are public. All are so new that no formula for their organization can be laid down. But it is clear that a community arts council should keep in close touch with the local government. It may be possible that an arts council could, in some instances, be organized as a municipal arts commission. It is in serving as a bridge between the local government and an arts commission—whether through formal statutory arrangement or informally—that a cultural officer can play a particularly constructive role in the development of the arts.

THE STATE ROLE

One of the most encouraging signs on the American cultural scene is the increasing concern of state governments with the arts. New York and North Carolina have led the way, with California now joining them. In all parts of the country these examples are being watched, and comparable initiatives considered or undertaken.

The states concerned themselves with social legislation before the federal government acted in this field. In the arts the states once more seem to be taking the lead. Here again their willingness to experiment, to try different solutions according to different circumstances, may serve them—and their citizens—well.

It is significant that New York and North Carolina, the first states to provide substantial direct support for the arts, did so from decidedly different political, social, and economic backgrounds. One state is northern and largely industrial and urban; the other is southern and largely rural and agricultural. In taking the lead as art patrons, they have demonstrated that no particular stage or form of state development is prerequisite to effective action.

The panel believes the principal role of state governments in regard to the performing arts is to see that presentations of high professional quality are made available to citizens throughout the state, particularly where local arts organizations cannot provide such opportunities. The range of programs that a state should consider includes: assessing statewide needs and making inventories of state and regional resources; supporting professional touring programs; providing technical assistance for local organizations; encouraging regional cooperation and development; developing the cultural programs within state educational institutions; removing tax burdens and legislative restrictions.

Assessing Statewide Needs

There are more than twenty state arts councils or commissions that have been authorized by legislative sanction or executive order. Not even half are beyond the paper stage of development. Their first step, once they are firmly established, is obviously to take a survey of needs and resources in the arts. If this is to be done well, some financial provision is necessary. In launching its Arts Commission in 1963, California provided it with an initial budget of $50,000 for preliminary study, with the expectation that larger state funds for support of the arts would be forthcoming when the work was done. Some states have not provided even preliminary funds; this omission can defeat an arts council or a state arts program almost before it begins.

Sponsoring Tours and Exchange Programs

Some smaller communities cannot generate audiences large enough to support anything like a regular season of professional performances. State governments can overcome this deficiency by sponsoring or helping to finance tours by high-quality professional organizations.

New York and North Carolina have developed different ways to supplement local resources by touring. A large portion of the funds of the New York State Council on the Arts is used to support tours by established professional performing groups and exhibitions of the visual arts. Local sponsors decide what they want and apply to the Council for assistance. The Council estimates what part of the cost can be covered by admissions or from other local sources and allocates funds to cover the balance. During 1963, at a cost of $168,000, this program provided 224 performances by fifty-seven companies that played in eighty-eight communities in the state.

In North Carolina, the largest appropriation for the performing arts ($75,000 for 1963–64) supports a single organization—the North Carolina Symphony. But it is really an appropriation for what is essentially a touring organization, with the orchestra receiving additional support from the localities it visits and the free use of public halls wherever available. In 1964, the Symphony played 129 concerts in fifty-four communities, including eighty-four special matinees for school children. The state also contracts with a professional company to perform excerpts from Shakespeare at high schools throughout the state.

Providing Technical Assistance

Arts organizations in smaller communities—both amateur and professional—frequently suffer from lack of expert technical assistance in performance, administration, and provision of physical facilities. The New York State Council on the Arts has taken a lead in overcoming this difficulty by making the services of expert technical consultants available to arts organizations. For instance:

In Oswego, the community theatre requested the Council's advice on the conversion of an old military building into a theatre and art gallery. The Council arranged for a member of its staff to advise on organization and administration, for a professional theatrical designer to help in adapting the building for both theatre and gallery uses, and for consultations with a lighting expert. In another case, the Council sent the manager of the summer dance programs in Central Park in New York City to assist a community dance group in Harlem to convert space into a theatre. At the request of the Utica Symphony Orchestra, the Council arranged for the Eastman School of Music quartet to hold a clinic and special rehearsals with the orchestra's string sections in an effort to strengthen them.

Toward Regional Cooperation in the Arts

In drafting legislation dealing with the arts, it is particularly important for the states not to place legal barriers in the way of regional cooperation. Many arts organizations quite naturally serve the interests of an area much larger than the state in which they are physically located. The Buffalo Philharmonic Orchestra, for instance, serves an area that includes communities outside New York State and, indeed, outside the United States. The Tyrone Guthrie Theatre in Minneapolis also draws its audiences from several surrounding states and Canada. Far from discouraging this sort of regionalism, states should encourage it. An audience drawn from a wide area spreads the burden of support and lessens the obligations placed on local residents. Moreover, the ability to lengthen a season through touring may, in the future, create higher artistic standards and, in the very long run, raise the cultural standards of vast regions or even the entire nation.

Developing the Arts in Education

In the field of specialized professional training, the state of North Carolina recently took a notable step of potential benefit to its whole region. In the absence of a private institution or the possibility of one, the legislature established a state-supported school of performing arts at the elementary school, high school, and college levels, provided that its initial annual contribution of $325,000 is matched by private funds for a period of five years. Afterward it is understood that the state will assume entire financial responsibility.

In order to bring the school to their city, more than five thousand citizens of Winston-Salem and several local foundations subscribed $1,015,000 for the construction of new dormitories and for the improvement of auditorium facilities in one of the city's three high schools. These facilities and twenty acres of land have been made available by the Winston-Salem school board. The school will open in September 1965, with 400 students, and its maximum enrollment of 600 will be reached two or three years later. Its launching constitutes an example of effective collaboration between private, state, and municipal enterprise in advancing the performing arts.

Removing Restrictive Burdens on Localities

Some state constitutions—including New York's and North Carolina's—require enabling legislation to permit cities or counties to give financial support to private organizations. Other state constitutions flatly prohibit direct municipal or county assistance to private organizations—a provision that is sometimes construed to apply to nonprofit arts organizations. The Washington State constitution, for example, has been very strictly interpreted in this area. In one case, a few years ago, the attorney general ruled that city funds could not be contributed to a nonprofit corporation that had been formed to construct and operate a community recreation center. The ruling also said that leasing to a private corporation, at nominal rental, property that had been a profitable source of income to the town "might possibly be construed as giving money or property in violation of the constitutional provision."

While there are various ways in which most cities and counties can comply with restrictions and still support arts organizations—by providing free administrative assistance and purchasing services—it is desirable to meet the issue head on and to take action to free the arts from categorical restrictions on direct support.

Advantages of State Arts Councils

New York and North Carolina have used different governmental mechanisms to support the arts. The New York State Council on the Arts was created under the leadership of Governor Nelson A. Rockefeller in 1960 to encourage appreciation of and participation in all the arts. The Council—fifteen members staffed by a full-time director and full-time and temporary assistants—receives a blanket appropriation ($534,219 in 1963–64). It allocates the funds in what the Council believes to be the most promising ways to serve its basic purpose.

In North Carolina, in contrast, the general procedure has been for the state legislature to make specific appropriations for arts projects, with the leadership in this process concentrated largely in the office of the governor.

Whether financial support for the performing arts via a state arts council as in New York or by specific legislative appropriations as in North Carolina is likely to be the more effective procedure necessarily depends in large degree on circumstances peculiar to the state involved. Governor Terry Sanford of North Carolina told this panel that the legislative background of his state and the situation presently prevailing there make legislative appropriations for specific projects a good mechanism for supporting the performing arts. It should be observed, however, that these circumstances include, perhaps pre-eminently, the presence of a governor who is vitally and effectively interested in having the performing arts well supported by the state.

As a general proposition, the panel believes that a state arts council, commission, or similar body, permanently constituted and strongly staffed, can provide elements of stability and continuity in support of the arts that may well be lost where the support depends primarily on continuity of individual leadership and legislative appropriations for specific projects. Most of the present state arts councils are still in the survey and recommendation stage of development, but as a mechanism to develop support for the performing arts some of them have demonstrated strengths that cannot generally be as well secured in any other way.

THE FEDERAL ROLE

In contrast to the numerous precedents for local and state government interest in the arts, the support and attention the federal government has given the performing arts—and, for that matter, the arts in general—has been largely incidental to some other purpose.

In the beginning leaders of the federal government stressed the importance of the arts in civilized society. It was Washington who observed that "the arts and sciences are essential to the prosperity of the state and to the ornament and happiness of human life." A century and a half passed, however, before the federal government first became deeply involved in the performing arts, and then as incidental to providing employment during the economically depressed thirties rather than as an affirmative artistic endeavor. In 1935, Congress established and financed the Works Progress Administration to create jobs on a large scale for the unemployed, and by Executive order the Federal Theatre Project was made part of the program.

Between 1936 and 1939, 63,728 performances were financed at a cost of slightly more than $46 million. However, the Federal Theatre Project was plagued in the halls of Congress. Of the 830 major titles produced by the project, 81—almost 10 percent—were criticized by congressmen or witnesses before congressional committees. In June 1939, in passing an appropriation of $1.75 billion for the Works Progress Administration, the House of Representatives made a specific proviso that none of the money could be spent on the Federal Theatre Project—a provision to which the Senate yielded, although it was actually willing to have the program continue.

A Place in the Government Structure

Despite this action, there has been increasing presidential advocacy of federal support for cultural activities and a growing number of congressional proposals to give effect to such a policy.

President Kennedy took pioneering steps when, in

March 1962, he appointed August Heckscher as his Special Consultant on the Arts. In April 1964, President Johnson also recognized the importance to the national government of fostering the arts by appointing Roger L. Stevens as his Special Assistant on the Arts to "organize and direct the Administration's cultural program."

Persistent congressional efforts culminated in the passage of a bill "To provide for the establishment of a National Council on the Arts to assist in the growth and development of the arts in the United States." Public Law 88–579 was signed by President Johnson on September 3, 1964, and provides for a chairman and a twenty-four-member arts council to be located in the Executive Office of the President. Among its duties are to:

> . . . recommend ways to maintain and increase the cultural resources of the United States . . . encourage private initiative in the arts . . . advise and consult with local, State, and Federal departments and agencies, on methods by which to coordinate existing resources and facilities . . . conduct studies and make recommendations with a view to formulating methods or ways by which creative activity and high standards and increased opportunities in the arts may be encouraged and promoted . . . and a greater appreciation and enjoyment of the arts by our citizens encouraged and developed.

This Council has been a long time coming, the first bill to create an organization of this kind having been introduced in Congress in 1877. In effect, the present bill gives congressional sanction to the Advisory Council on the Arts that President Kennedy created by Executive order in June 1963, but to which he made no appointments before his death. The advantage of creating an arts council through congressional action is obvious. Its position is more secure, its prestige probably higher, and its ability to stimulate action greater than if the Council had been created through Executive action. In short, the bill's passage is a most favorable omen.

The panel supports the development of a National Council on the Arts and urges that sufficient funds be provided to carry out the responsibilities assigned to it by Congress. The annual budget of $150,000 for the Council, which is presently authorized in the legislation, is not as large as would seem necessary to fulfill its duties, and the actual appropriation for the Council for fiscal year 1964–65 was only $50,000. Lack of adequate funds could seriously inhibit, for example, its surveying and coordinating efforts.

Strengthening and Utilizing Present Programs

In the legislation establishing a National Council on the Arts, its chairman is specifically charged with the responsibility for advising the President with respect to the activities of the federal government in the arts. There are some that are directly related to the arts, others that indirectly affect them, and some, like taxation policies and copyright laws, that can encourage or restrict the development of the arts.

Direct Commitment to the Arts. There are a few continuing federal programs that recognize and provide opportunities for the professional performing arts. In the aggregate they are of slight magnitude and are largely dependent on private gifts. Among these programs are the literary and music programs of the Library of Congress and the National Gallery, historic pageants held with the cooperation of the National Park Service, and artistic performances in Washington occasionally sponsored by members of the Cabinet and by the White House. In August 1964, for the first time in its history, Congress passed an appropriation of $25,000 for public service concerts to be given by the National Symphony Orchestra. This, in effect, was an adoption of the principle of municipal support for the arts.

The Office of Education has established an Arts and Humanities Branch to strengthen general arts education and improve the level of public appreciation. It is formulating programs and research projects aimed at discovering talent, improving teaching techniques, using new educational media, and encouraging professional performances in schools. The staff includes a director and specialists in music, museum education, theatre education, art education, and the humanities. In addition, there are legislative proposals for a much more extensive involvement of the Office of Education in the arts, one of which is to create within the Office of Education a National Institute of Arts and Humanities. There are important possibilities for encouraging the development of the arts in the stirrings in the Office of Education. Its programs should not be considered as alternative but rather supplemental to those of the National Council on the Arts.

The John F. Kennedy Center for the Performing Arts, in Washington, D.C., is the federal government's most direct commitment to these arts. As contrasted with the facilities provided by the Library of Congress, the National Gallery, or various departmental auditoriums, the Kennedy Center will provide halls specially designed for concert, opera, and drama.

In 1958, Congress chartered what was then known as the National Cultural Center, making a direct gift of the land. President Eisenhower appointed the first board of trustees. After President Kennedy's assassination, Congress constituted the Center as a memorial to him and voted $15.5 million to supplement private funds for buildings and parking facilities. Thus, there has been substantial and increasing investment in this undertaking.

The artistic direction of the Kennedy Center as an institution of the performing arts is not yet clear. A standard of performance on its stages equal to the distinguished character of the structure is essential to make the Center a worthy memorial to President Kennedy.

Incidental but Direct Support. There are several areas in which the federal government directly supports the arts, but only incidentally to fufilling some other purpose.

The Cultural Presentations Program, which since 1954 has carried an appropriation of about $2.5 million a year, is an international cultural showcase of the West. Under this program, administered by the Department of State, individual artists and performing groups—both professional and amateur—are sent on overseas tours. So are athletic and sports groups. Since its inception this program has assisted almost 300 presentations or tours abroad by individual artists and groups. During the 1963–64 season, for example, 18 groups (11 professional and 7 academic) and 6 individuals totaling 647 performing artists appeared in 246 cities and 90 countries. People in areas as remote as the Congo and Cambodia have been able to enjoy performances by distinguished American artists and talented academic groups.

The United States Information Agency's overseas staff is generally responsible for all local arrangements for programing these cultural presentations and for promotional activities in conjunction with the tours. Basic press, radio, and film materials sent from Washington are adapted and placed among overseas media for advance promotion. In addition to its support of the Cultural Presentations Program, USIA widely distributes recordings of American music and lectures and other material concerning the arts in the United States. The Agency also is instrumental in obtaining rights for foreign performances of American music as well as amateur productions of plays.

There is an artistic *quid pro quo* for Americans in the cultural exchanges agreement between the United States and the Soviet Union. Since these performing arts exchanges began in 1955, more than fifteen major American groups have been sent on tour in the U.S.S.R. under contract with the Soviet State Concert Agency. In exchange, Soviet groups, including the Moscow Philharmonic, the Leningrad Philharmonic, the Bolshoi Ballet, and the Leningrad Kirov Ballet have visited the United States.

The international presentations programs should be continued, even if cold war pressures decline. What was begun with the arts only indirectly in mind could well become a major way of promoting American achievements, as well as increasing international understanding, if emphasis is placed on selecting the best work of American playwrights, composers, choreographers, actors, musicians, and dancers. Maintenance of the highest standards and insulation of the program from interference on narrow political grounds cannot be too strongly stressed. It should be noted that the limited availability of funds largely prevents the use of theatre groups or symphony orchestras.

The entertainment and education programs sponsored by the Defense Department involve the performing arts quite extensively. The Armed Forces Professional Entertainment Branch, charged with providing live entertainment to military personnel stationed at remote and isolated bases, takes about eighty-five units overseas annually to carry out this commission. The Defense Department usually pays transportation and living costs, while the performers receive no compensation or are paid from private contributions. In addition, the various service bands provide concert programs for military and civilian audiences in many countries. The armed services also sponsor performing arts programs by members of the services as part of their recreational-educational program.

The programs of the Defense Department in the performing arts are mainly directed to morale building rather than advancement of these arts or the provision of superior cultural opportunities for Americans in uniform. They are also of less material benefit to the professional performing arts than their magnitude might suggest. In many cases professional artists receive less than full compensation, and sometimes none at all, and service bands in certain circumstances pay no royalties for the music they play, as is the case with the music used for concerts given in the Library of Congress.

Indirect Support of Value. There are also federal programs unrelated in origin to the arts that could give great assistance to them if administered with this possibility in mind. The Urban Renewal Program, which was established to eliminate and prevent slums, can be of help in providing suitable and strategically located land for new facilities for the performing arts. The Urban Renewal Administration will approve the inclusion of auditoriums, civic and cultural centers, concert halls, and theatres on urban renewal project land when such uses are included in a community's Urban Renewal Plan. However, no urban renewal funds are available for construction of these facilities. Performing facilities already built or planned in urban renewal project areas include Lincoln Center in New York City, the Arena Stage in Washington, D.C., a theatre in the Charles Center project in Baltimore, a Civic Arts Center in Asheville, North Carolina, concert halls and theatres in Chicago and Pittsburgh, the Drexel Institute Activity Center in Philadelphia, a Civic Auditorium in Grand Rapids, Michigan, a concert hall in Milwaukee, "little theatres" in Chicago and in Monterey, California, and a Civic Auditorium in Boston.

In the federal public works and community development programs, auditoriums, theatres, and cultural centers are not specifically excluded, but very few projects of this type have been aided. There has been some assistance to civic auditoriums, though little attention has generally been paid to making them suitable for dramatic and musical performances. This neglect can be rectified without reducing the ability of these projects to provide employment and stimulate economic growth. The potential can actually be increased by competent and continuous concern for the cultural activities of the community.

Nonprofit arts organizations also could be helped by modifying the policies now governing the disposal of surplus federal property—real and personal—which runs into many millions of dollars annually. Under present law, nonprofit educational institutions are among those that may acquire this property on a free or low-cost basis. Nonprofit museums, theatres, orchestras, and cultural and arts centers, all of which have major educational functions, should be made equally eligible.

In recent years the fact-collecting agencies of the federal government have begun to pay more attention to the arts. Two publications of the Department of Commerce, the *Census of Business,* taken every five years, and the survey of Personal Consumption Expenditures, which appears annually in the July issue of the monthly *Survey of Current Business,* include statistics about the performing arts, as does the *Occupational Outlook Handbook,* published by the Department of Labor. In the *Survey of Current Business,* however, the data is included in the category "amusement and recreation services." But reasonably reliable, comprehensive, and up-to-date figures about such elemental matters as numbers of performing groups, types of facilities, character of services, and sources of financial support remain to be assembled. Yet the Bureau of Census records, for example, give for every county in the nation statistics such as the percentage of houses with plumbing facilities, television sets, air conditioning, and telephones.

The arts can be encouraged also by government recognition of outstanding individual contributions to their development. President Kennedy took a helpful step in this direction in February 1963, when he broadened the scope and purpose of awards of the Medal of Freedom (the highest civil honor awarded by the federal government) to include artistic and cultural leaders. The award had originally been established for meritorious civilian service in World War II. There is occasion, however, to develop further awards for distinguished service in the arts—awards roughly comparable in their field to the National Medal of Science and the Fermi and Lawrence Awards for outstanding contributions to the development of atomic energy.

The panel believes that existing federal arts programs, limited though they are, can be strengthened and that federal programs indirectly affecting the arts should be administered with a greater awareness of their cultural implications. The National Council on the Arts can perform a highly useful function in keeping all the federal policies and programs affecting the arts under continuing review. Its chairman, who will generally serve also as the President's Special Assistant on the Arts, has the additional day-to-day opportunity of representing the cause of the arts at the point where administrative decisions are being made. His White House office is strategically situated to keep him in contact with the various government departments and agencies. To be effective his office requires adequate staffing and assurance of full support.

Encouragement, Not Restriction. It frequently is argued that while the performing arts receive virtually no direct financial support, the federal government is actually one of their major financial benefactors, by making contributions to nonprofit performing arts organizations tax deductible. There is validity in this position, and it emphasizes both the responsibilities of the arts organizations so benefited and the responsibility of the federal government to protect its interest in their successful development.

At the same time, however, the federal government imposes special tax burdens on presentation of the performing arts. This is most notably true of the commercial theatre, subject to a 10 percent excise tax on admissions. The commercial theatre's artistic and economic future is vital to the performing arts, and it should be spared the burden of the admissions tax. It is a serious reflection upon the validity of the theatre as one of the most significant of art forms. In complaining about the federal excise tax of 10 percent on musical instruments, professional musicians observe that no other worker pays such a tax on his tools.

The federal government, by omission rather than commission, imposes other special burdens on the performing arts and artists. One of these is the provision of the copyright law that permits the jukebox industry to escape royalty payments for its use of copyrighted music. In 1909, when the record business was in its infancy, Congress revised the copyright law and exempted performances of copyrighted music that were not public and not for profit from obligation to pay royalties. A specific clause was written into the law exempting owners of coin-operated machines from any obligation to pay royalties for the public performance of music. As a result, after the jukebox industry buys the records it uses, no royalties are paid for repeated playings.

It is estimated that the gross income from approximately half a million jukeboxes is close to half a billion dollars a year. If the jukebox industry were subjected to royalty payments for playing copyrighted music, the musical arts as a whole could be given a substantial economic lift. One way has been pointed by the American Society of Composers, Authors and Publishers (ASCAP) and Broadcast Music, Inc. (BMI). In 1963, they collected a total of over $50 million for bulk licensing of all users of music other than the jukebox industry. Most of the music played was, of course, popular music, but ASCAP and BMI have developed workable formulas enabling them to distribute to serious composers a larger proportion than a strictly prorated share of the royalties they collect. Another possibility might be a provision requiring that royalties be channeled into a fund similar to the Recording Industries Music Performance Trust Funds administered by a trustee representing the public.

There are other ways by which revision of the federal copyright law could better protect the creative artist. One of the most important of these is extension of the time span of copyright protection—now a twenty-eight-year original period with a renewal period of twenty-eight years—to a term comparable to that prevailing in England and most of Europe, which is the author's lifetime plus fifty years. At present, many elderly artists are in the curious position of outliving the royalties on their early works just at the time of life when this income may be most valuable to them.

An equally serious problem, particularly pressing for composers and playwrights, is the need for protection against the pirating of material through the use of copying machines, which have the potential of allowing the unscrupulous to avoid paying performance royalties by avoiding purchase of material from sources that pay author royalties. A borrowed copy of a play and a copying machine are all that is necessary these days to pirate a work.

But perhaps the most serious threat is the current advocacy to exempt educational institutions from the obligation to pay royalties for the performance of musical, dramatic, and literary works. Some educational associations are seeking to gain a very broad exemption in the revision of the copyright law on the use of artistic creation, extending even to an exemption for mimeographed material used by a teacher in a classroom. But their efforts are focused on gaining freedom from royalties and control by the author of material used by educational television. Although educational television, in its initial stages, clearly deserves concessions and intelligent cooperation in its development by artists, there seems no reason why it should receive blanket exemption from the payment of reasonable fees. Were it to receive this exemption—indeed, if any educational institution were to receive it—artists would once more be in the position of being forced to provide a partial subsidy for the general cultural and intellectual development of the nation.

In discussing the federal government's taxation policies affecting the arts, it has been suggested that a tax of some sort be imposed upon the television and radio industries to help the performing arts. Sometimes the proposal is to tax the gross annual income of these industries, which has been running over $2 billion a year. Sometimes it is to levy a transfer tax on the sales of radio and television stations, which, over the past ten years, have amounted to about $1.06 billion in total sales. Sometimes it is to apply a licensing fee on the station owner.

The justification presented for a special tax on television and radio is that the airwaves belong to the public, and the public is entitled to payment when an exclusive right to exploit them for private profit is granted.

The argument is also made that, as a matter of equity, the television and radio industries should contribute to the support and development of those sources of art and talent on which their success depends in substantial measure. The validity of this argument, however, is questioned by the industries on the grounds that they probably contribute as much, if not more, to the performing arts than they receive, since they provide well-paid employment opportunities, play an important role in the development of audiences for these arts, and through their public service programs subsidize performances.

There are precedents for directing excise taxes or use fees to the support of related activities. In the United States, for example, the receipts from a manufacturer's excise tax on fishing and hunting equipment is allocated to fish and wildlife conservation programs; marine fuel taxes and admission fees to federal recreation areas are earmarked for the Land and Water Conservation Fund. In Austria, a tax is levied on admissions to motion picture theatres for the support of the performing arts. In Italy, funds derived from a tax on all public shows, sporting events, and betting games are used for financial support of the arts. In nearly all Western European countries, radio and television set owners must pay the government a tax that is used to support network programs, many of which are provided, of course, by performing arts groups.

Determining the advisability of imposing a tax on the television and radio industries for the benefit of the performing arts is a complex matter, one not within the purview of this study, and one on which this panel has not taken a position.

Direct Financial Assistance

There is an increasing demand for direct federal financial support for the performing arts, and it seems safe to forecast that this demand will continue to grow. Hence, there is urgent occasion for searching study on a continuing basis by the National Council on the Arts to determine the most desirable types of federal support and the most desirable ways of providing them.

Many possibilities have been suggested through the years. One kind of support would be to make matching grants for adequate physical facilities, of which there is a grave shortage for the professional performing arts. Another would be to make matching grants to the states, which would administer aid to their arts organizations. Still another would be embodied in national education programs to improve the quality of training in the arts and to increase popular appreciation for them, which, viewed in the longer perspective, is essential to their economic salvation.

In considering the establishment of an agency to administer assistance for the arts, the merits of various types of organizations ranging in character from that of the National Science Foundation, to the Office of Education, to the National Academy of Sciences, to a Cabinet rank department would all have to be carefully reviewed.

There are also many possible techniques for providing aid to be considered. The matching grant principle, which has been extensively used in recent years to provide federal support for enterprises closely related to the arts, such as higher education, has much to recommend it. There are ample precedents for varying the percentage of matching required of recipients. This arrangement is particularly appropriate in the case of the arts, where development in the states and regions is very uneven, creating striking differences between organizations as to their need for financial help by the federal government and their capacity to use it effectively.

Study of government support for the performing arts by the National Council on the Arts would serve to make it clear that the place where an arts organization is physically located has little bearing on the scope of its artistic expression. While Lincoln Center, the San Francisco Ballet, and the Boston Symphony Orchestra are physically located in New York City, San Francisco, and Boston, they are all in fact organizations of national significance. The same is true of other major arts organizations over the country that carry out programs of the highest quality, commanding national—indeed international—attention and respect. Hence, if support were to be routed to these organizations from Washington, its immediate destination would be local, but its ultimate effect would be to advance a national resource. This would be particularly true if we develop and improve facilities all over the nation that will encourage tours and exchanges between arts organizations.

To Protect Freedom and Promote Quality. The danger of having federal interference with artistic freedom follow federal financial support, unless there are proper safeguards, is no mere bugaboo. Our country has grown in artistic sophistication in the quarter century since the Federal Theatre Project fell victim to politics, but this does not mean that the problem of protecting artistic freedom is to be brushed aside lightly.

Perhaps an even greater danger of support by any level of government is the encouragement of mediocrity. If public funds for the arts were spread among all the arts organizations regardless of quality, if the making of grants to arts organizations becomes a matter of political logrolling, a Rivers and Harbors pork barrel for sophisticates, then improvement in the quality of the arts would be negligible—no matter how much is spent.

There are, however, effective ways, well tested both in this country and abroad, by which financial help from the national government can be administered while full artistic freedom is protected and quality is encouraged. The operation of the Arts Council of Great Britain demonstrates one such way. It is a partnership of private and government initiative. Parliament provides the appropriations, and the Council, composed of specially qualified private citizens and aided by expert panels, distributes the support—without parliamentary interference. This arrangement, not unlike that provided by the University Grants Committee for British colleges and universities, combines a bulwark for freedom with qualified artistic guidance and the mobilization of public resources for the development of the arts. There are other arrangements in Western Europe, where the serious performing arts almost uniformly receive heavy support from public funds, that serve effectively to safeguard artistic freedom. A study of the professional performing arts in Europe, commissioned for this panel, disclosed virtually no complaint that public funds had impaired artistic freedom.

In our own country, the National Science Foundation and the National Institutes of Health have demonstrated that massive federal support can be used effectively without compromising intellectual and scientific freedom and quality. A series of expert panels helps the National Science Foundation to pass on the financing of projects within their special fields of competence. Interested congressmen are systematically kept informed of the recommendations of these panels, a procedure that has been found to reduce temptation to interfere with operations.

Given time and study, it would seem reasonable to assume that machinery can also be developed to provide protection to artistic freedom while giving the arts access to such federal financial support as may be deemed desirable.

Matching Grants for Capital Equipment. The panel believes that for the present federal aid for arts organizations, apart from the minuscule amount now available, can be most effectively provided through matching grants to meet the capital needs of arts organizations.

In urging that grants be restricted at present for assistance to building, it seems appropriate to point out that we need far more general experience in making grants to arts organizations. Matching grants for capital development can help provide this experience. Grants for other purposes related to the arts can be considered as the nation's cultural program develops.

Meantime, we will have made a contribution toward solving a basic problem in the performing arts—the need for adequate physical facilities. The record demonstrates that the federal government, by the judicious use of the matching principle, can stimulate increased state and local, public and private support. But a great educational effort is needed to obtain even the matching grants for capital improvement proposed here, and the National Council on the Arts can be of inestimable value in this regard.

In favoring federal matching grants to meet the capital requirements of arts organizations, the panel bases its judgment in part on a body of experience broadly applicable to arts organizations. The Library Services Act was amended in 1964 to include aid for construction as well as services. It had been found that although libraries qualify as public works programs, the existing restrictions, plus competition from projects deemed of more urgent economic necessity, meant that library needs were not being met. In another area, the federal government is empowered to stimulate the creation of educational television facilities.

Grants-in-aid on a matching basis were authorized in 1962 to the extent of $32 million over a five-year period. Another key problem has been to give our institutions of higher education some desperately needed financial help, but to keep the risk of federal interference with the educational process at a minimum. It was found that the best way to do this was to provide matching grants for capital equipment, leaving the educational process strictly alone. The same general procedure is applicable to arts organizations, where the protection of artistic freedom is as essential as scientific or academic freedom.

In summary, the panel concludes that while private support should remain dominant, the federal government—together with state and local governments—should give strong support to the arts, including the performing arts, by appropriate recognition of their importance, by direct and indirect encouragement, and by financial cooperation.

8
Organization and Management of the Arts

Too many people believe that a simple infusion of more money will solve all the problems of the performing arts in this country. But money is, in the last analysis, a neutral object, a tool. It has no capacity for vision; this must be supplied by men. Money can be poured into any project, but if it is not used wisely and imaginatively, it is money wasted. We will not realize our objective—a flourishing world of the performing arts in America—unless those who guide our performing arts organizations demonstrate a capacity to see beyond present crises and plan for the expanding future. *As talent is needed to create and perform a work of art, so equal talent—though of a different sort—is needed to create and govern the institutions that provide the settings for these arts. It is for this reason the panel believes it essential for an arts organization to have an effective board of trustees and competent management in addition to talented artistic direction.*

THE GOVERNING BOARD

Whenever performing arts organizations reach the stage of development where permanence is sought, they almost invariably become nonprofit corporations, headed by a board of trustees vested with the responsibility of maintaining and expanding the organization.

This board has certain obvious functions: to determine the larger objectives of the organization, to retain the best available artistic direction and business management, and, having accomplished the latter, to back their judgment when the inevitable conflicts with artists or with elements in the community arise. In fulfilling these responsibilities, the board has a pressing obligation to make certain the institution has financial stability, for without it there can be little hope of attaining either the long-range or the short-term goals the board may decide upon.

The actual selection of goals is crucial. Too many arts organizations seem to live from minute to minute or, at best, from year to year. A careful step-by-step plan, projected over a number of years, is essential to the arts organization, as is the selection of ultimate goals that are realistic in terms of the needs and desires of the community served. In the selection of intelligent goals the board can be of great assistance to managers and artistic directors, who may be strangers to the community, without intimate knowledge of its tastes or its capacity for artistic growth. In this connection it should be noted that lofty but impossible goals are easy to proclaim; practical goals, representing the highest level of achievement attainable with available resources, are the products of the most difficult and sustained effort on the part of the board and management—artistic and business. The story is true of the board members who would have been happy to disband the orchestra on being faced for the first time with a five-year budget based on the plan they themselves had developed.

Goals cannot be the product of snap judgments nor are they likely to result from the deliberations of board members who regard their posts as merely a social honor. Indeed, as the number and complexity of arts organizations grow, board membership is becoming much more arduous than in decades past. Yet board recruitment remains much too casual in most organizations. Meticulous auditioning procedures are used for second violinists, members of the opera chorus, and bit players in the theatre, but people about whom practically nothing is known often are chosen to be trustees. Board members should be as carefully screened as performers, and procedures for rotating membership should be considered. The potential for serious and prolonged damage to the organization is as high in the board room as on the stage.

It should also be borne clearly in mind that, with the increase of interest and the base of support for the arts broadening, a board should be more widely representative of the community than is generally true today. There is simple common sense in this principle. Board members informally representing many different publics within a community can be effective mobilizers of audiences and support from new sources. Beyond this, valuable personal skills are added to the board when members are recruited from the arts, from education, from the mass media, labor, and government. Too many boards continue to draw members from a relatively narrow segment of the community. In so doing, they take on the character of a closed club, with disastrous effect on their ability to develop audiences and to appeal for support from the community at large. They also run the risk of a narrow parochialism of outlook that can hinder all planning and growth.

It is particularly important that board members be receptive to change and innovation. Too often the relationship between a board and the artistic director of an arts organization deteriorates into a squabble between traditionalists who "know what they like" and artists who insist on pressing outward against the boundaries of the usual. A certain amount of tension is undoubtedly healthy, but board members will sacrifice some of the strength of their position—and the respect of their artist colleagues—if they do not bring to these discussions of aesthetic questions a degree of knowledgeability and sophistication. We have already noted that a great need in the performing arts is for a higher and higher degree of cooperation between arts organizations. In this context the modern board member must be prepared, on occasion, to sacrifice some of his organization's autonomy for the greater good of his community or his region's cultural development, or, indeed, for its own long-term gain. Again, sophistication and flexibility are needed if board members are to seize these opportunities for growth.

In this country, the artistic leadership has frequently been responsible for the very creation of the organization. Many orchestras were founded on the initiative of a conductor; most dance companies were established solely by the conviction of a choreographer that his works merited performance; the impetus toward permanent professional theatres in recent years has often derived from the men and women who serve as directors. The artistic leaders have even reversed the usual sequence and chosen their boards and business managers to take responsibilities from their overburdened shoulders. Such reversal, however, should not be accepted as changing the respective roles of trustees, manager, and artistic director. The presence of a strong founding personality actually places an extra obligation on the board of directors. An organization has a way of achieving a life of its own, of extending beyond the interest span or the talents or, perhaps, the very life of the individual largely responsible for its creation. The board has a distinct obligation to develop within itself the strength to carry on after the founder departs and to create machinery to assure a smooth transition of power when that event occurs. Similarly, the founder-artist has an obligation to his community, even perhaps to his own place in history, to see that "his" board has the strength and intelligence to carry on after he leaves.

The Chairman and His Board

Special qualifications for the chairman of a board of trustees range from ability to conduct a meeting with due regard for *Robert's Rules of Order* (a capacity that is not a natural endowment, although many seem to think it is) to capacity to mediate between his lay and artistic associates on matters calling for supreme tact and diplomacy. He is the bridge between the management and the board and between various groups on the board. As the leader of a part-time avocational group, he must also expect to put in far more time for the organization than the other trustees generally do.

Serious consideration should be given by the large organizations to the currently almost untried procedure of having a full-time paid president or chief executive. No industry with a budget comparable in size to those of a growing number of orchestras would think of operating with voluntary leisure-time leadership. The chairman must also have good, well-organized help from the board. Appropriate committee structures necessarily vary from one art to another, and from one stage of development to another. In all cases, however, a strong executive committee capable of moving with dispatch is essential for effective performance. So, too, is the limitation of committees to those that clearly have an important role to perform such as finance, development, community service.

The flow of command and control should be clearcut and the organization and procedures of the board readily understandable and practical. In theory, the articles of incorporation and the bylaws of nonprofit arts organizations should be something of a blueprint of their broad purposes and procedures. But a study of these documents for symphony orchestras discloses that all too often they fail to provide an adequate or accurate statement of their organization's purpose.

The Board's Relationship to Management

Governing boards will constantly be faced with problems that can be solved only by deliberate, systematic, and wholesale delegation of responsibilities. They must therefore depend, to a frightening extent, on the counsel they receive. Success in the extraordinarily complicated field of the performing arts depends on the good will and mutual trust of all concerned. This derives from thorough understanding of the common goals to be sought and from mutual respect for areas of responsibility in the struggle to attain them.

Although effective trustees are bound to work continuously with their artistic directors and business managers, they do not meddle in artistic direction and business management. For them there is profound wisdom in the injunction: Do your best to see that the organization is good, that it is well manned, and that it runs smoothly—but don't try to run it.

As part of its primary responsibility for raising funds and spending them, the board must see that orderly business procedures are maintained and that money is available for maximum efficiency of operation. It should require that management submit periodic financial and progress reports, that sound bookkeeping and accounting procedures be followed, that annual audits be made, and that the organization have maximum financial protection.

Toward their artistic directors and business managers, the trustees have a critical responsibility no less crucial than seeing that they are well selected in the first place and working with them to develop and carry out basic policy: It is the responsibility of backing them up when necessary. All trustees are necessarily involved in the defense of artistic freedom, although this responsibility varies from one performing art to another. It is perhaps a more apparent and complex problem in the theatre, which frequently deals with highly inflammatory matters of morality and ideology. But it may also arise in the symphony orchestra field on the question of how much contemporary music is to be played even when sufficient funds are available. Surely no one should accept trusteeship of any performing arts organization who is not willing, on occasion, to stand embattled in defense of management's freedom to fulfill what it conceives to be its artistic mission. The defense, however, can be both simplified and made more effective by being an expression of a broad and firmly held basic policy rather than a catch-as-catch-can improvisation arising from the immediate issue at hand.

ARTISTIC DIRECTION

The task of selecting an artistic director is perhaps the most critical a board of trustees faces. The artistic director sets the standards of production, and artistic results can be no better than the quality of artistic direction. His duties are many and complicated.

Selection of Artists

Selection of artists is one of the most difficult responsibilities of the artistic director. In this process the director must come to terms with the star system. This question is, of course, closely allied to the question of artistic standards, but it also has economic aspects that cannot be overlooked. To engage a star is obviously to increase operating costs, though increased box office revenue frequently more than offsets these costs.

As a rule—to which, of course, there are notorious exceptions—a star's fame rests on superior talent and accomplishment. Therefore, a star's presence should insure higher quality performance. His presence may also lend cachet to the organization. But each artistic director must decide whether in the long run the star system is good for the institution.

Perhaps the most valuable form of stardom toward which an organization may aspire is that the company in and of itself have the power to draw the public to it. When this takes place, one may find that individual stars will be attracted to it too. The New York City Ballet, to mention but one example, lists all of its dancers in alphabetical order; yet an Erik Bruhn will give up personal billing for the sake of dancing with a stellar company.

For an arts institution to reach stardom requires time. Meanwhile, a policy of featuring guest artists, so long as their salaries do not ruin the budget or destroy the institution's potential for development on its own merits, may be necessary. But the artistic director who builds his program around visiting personalities is not giving adequate thought to the final objective—the day when the organization itself, not the names it hires, will attract the public.

Maintenance of Artistic Standards

The artistic director—the conductor, the stage director, the choreographer—through his competence, leadership, and imagination is the largest single factor in determining the morale and creative contribution of an artistic enterprise. Save in the orchestra world, where the conductor is in single artistic control, there must be a continuous merging and cooperation of talents—the director with the designer, with the choreographer, with all of those on stage who have important roles to play. If collaboration fails at any point, the quality of the entire effort may deteriorate.

But it is the artistic director who is finally responsible for the quality of performance, so it follows that he must maintain conditions from which high standards derive. What, generally, are these conditions?

Well-Trained Artists. The capable artistic director can sometimes weld a coherent musical or theatrical entity out of players with a wide diversity of backgrounds. But not even the finest can go beyond a certain point with ill-trained talent. The education and experience of the ensemble, individually and as a whole, are crucial elements in determining standards of performance.

Rehearsal Time. Most critical in the preparation of new and unfamiliar works, insufficient rehearsal hours can likewise damage with almost equal force the standard repertory. Few artists ever *feel* adequately rehearsed, but it is too often true in fact as well.

Length of Season. Quality thrives on practice and sustained performance. It can scarcely grow in a season that is nothing but a limited engagement or a scattered handful of performances. On the other hand, a full-year contract has drawbacks for many artists who feel that leisure—for contemplation, for study, for work they cannot accomplish during the hectic activity of "the season"—is a necessity for personal growth. As seasons lengthen and rehearsal and performance demands squeeze out "refreshing" activities essential to artistic health, it will be necessary to find a balance between continuity and variety, between holding a group together and providing free time for the individual. Perhaps an adaptation of the academic practice of the sabbatical would prove effective.

Compensation of Performers. Whatever the size of the group or the length of its season, an ill-paid performer is a dissatisfied performer. The size of the pocketbook also affects the adequacy of the instruments orchestral musicians can afford or be provided. This is an important building block in the total structure, especially since the problem may occur just below the level of the finest orchestras. For a musician, capital outlays for some instruments can represent the savings of a lifetime.

Physical Facilities. Many a performance might as well go unheard and unseen as to play in halls so ungrateful to sound and sight that players and audience alike have trouble perceiving a total effect. Other facilities, as they relate to the artists' comfort and convenience—adequate warm-up space for musicians and dancers, well-lighted dressing rooms for actors—can likewise be subtle contributors to the total health of the ensemble.

Audience. Only at its peril does an artistic director ignore his audience's taste. This is a delicate and difficult measurement to make, not unlike the statesman's: How to lead forward, but not too fast. An audience's knowledge and ability to appreciate affects the product. A conductor and his orchestra, a director and his cast, a choreographer and his dancers know perfectly well whether they are liked and understood, and they respond with their best when it is their best that the audience clearly wants and expects.

Each of these conditions is to an extent controllable by trustees and management, artistic and business. Each decision carries a price tag and each requires judgment, knowledge, and taste, in order that proper decisions may be arrived at by all concerned. It is essential, therefore, that artistic and business management work in true partnership, the director respecting the manager's concerns, and vice versa, and the trustees respecting both. Only a smoothly functioning team, in which each of these elements complements the others, can create a strong arts organization.

It would be unrealistic to think that adequate resources for all these objectives are obtainable by all organizations, especially in the early stages of development. It would be foolish, for example, for the conductor of the average community orchestra to demand from his orchestra a level of performance exceeding the competence of the musicians. The real challenge is to strive for an ever closer balance between the actual and the attainable and to make measurable progress toward the time when all conditions of quality can be considered relevant in planning future programs. If the artistic standards an organization sets for itself do not rise steadily upward, neither will quality, and performance will be doomed to spiritless mediocrity.

MANAGEMENT

Resourceful business and administrative leadership is a necessary element in the successful development of the performing arts. This is true of more firmly established organizations like symphony orchestras as well as it is of those, like repertory theatre and dance companies, that are in the early stages of growth. (Indeed, it might be said that until management does enter and take firm hold, the dance world will remain as inchoate and economically insecure as it is today.)

Too often the dilettante mentality—belief that all that is needed for success is talented artists—prevails. But a good orchestra, a good theatre, a good opera or dance group cannot be established or run by well-wishing volunteers.

Good business brains and performance are essential to the successful operation of these organizations, but more than these are required, for the problems are unique. Artistic judgments defying business calculations enter at every step. In the profit-seeking business world there are clearcut measures of effectiveness: the income account and the balance sheet. For the nonprofit arts organization there is no such measure. There are no profits, and although a diminishing deficit might *seem* to indicate effective business management, this is not necessarily the case. It might simply reflect an increasing failure to meet artistic obligations.

What constitutes a good manager in this field? He has been described by an authority on the subject as a man "who must be knowledgeable in the art with which he is concerned, an impresario, labor negotiator, diplomat, educator, publicity and public relations expert, politician, skilled businessman, a social sophisticate, a servant of the community, a tireless leader—becomingly humble before authority—a teacher, a tyrant, and a continuing student of the arts." It is obvious that artistic knowledge of the field itself is not the only qualification for a successful manager. Indeed, some excellent managers have come from other fields and obtained their orientation in the arts on the job.

Managers as Skilled Businessmen

Let us examine one or two of these qualifications in detail. A "skilled businessman" functioning as manager of a performing arts organization will be expected to exhibit a high degree of analytical ability as well as the mechanical ability to carry out established business routines. With no profit ledger to measure success, other benchmarks must be observed.

Adequate accounting procedures go far beyond the record of cash intake and outgo and protection against dishonesty. A skilled manager also possesses the ability to prepare and present systematic reports of business operations that will give to those who are not masters in this field a broad understanding of the true picture and assure the board that administration is in accordance with approved policies and budget.

Not only is clearly presented, straightforward financial information important for the board as a guide to administration, it can also serve to improve relations with contributors—especially foundations and corporations—all levels of government, and, indeed, with unions. Too often, hiding facts whose publication would uncover an arts organization's sorry financial predicament, or even reveal unexpected affluence, works to its long-term disadvantage.

Perhaps because of their chronic condition of financial insecurity, arts organizations are notoriously adhesive to long-established methods of conducting business operations. Frequently these methods are as wasteful and inefficient as they are well intended. A good manager develops a deeply ingrained impatience with conducting business operations as they have been conducted simply because "that's the way it's always been done."

Managers as Labor Negotiators

The role of the general manager in the field of labor relations evolves from his responsibility to cope with a wide range of personnel problems.

While some unions on occasion impose restrictions on arts organizations, there are also occasions when unions have made lifesaving concessions to encourage and stimulate development. For example, the American Guild of Musical Artists, whose members include dancers and singers, has recognized that modern dance has such a small audience and is so imperfectly established as a way of life that application of standard union regulations is out of the question. It has made numerous concessions and in fact sponsored several talent showcases. It has similarly recognized the problems of choral singers. The off-Broadway theatre has also benefited from union cooperation, but as it grows finds the craft unions tightening their regulations. The stagehands and musicians have been particularly uncompromising in their dealings with theatrical managements. In the theatre one finds as well the largest number of abuses—featherbedding and needless extra charges such as those for standby musicians who never play.

Symphony orchestras and opera companies also have had serious union difficulties, widely publicized in recent seasons. The opera is especially vulnerable, since a management like the Metropolitan's must deal with some fourteen separate unions. Wage scale increases and other benefits granted to one union are bound to affect the others as well.

The difficulties in relationships between management and labor in the performing arts are undoubtedly aggravated by the fact that the supply of performers is generally larger than the demand for their services, that the seasonal nature of most organizations in the field often creates intolerable hardships because of intermittent employment and resulting inadequate salaries, and that adequate funds for support of the arts organization are difficult to raise.

It should be clearly understood that these conditions will not be solved by an attitude that assumes the artist should subsidize the arts by working for the lowest possible fee. Nor, on the other hand, is an answer to be found in union practices that are detrimental to the long-run growth of the arts.

The employment provided by a nonprofit organization should not differ in principle from that provided by a commercial operation. Too often, however, unions do not adequately take into account the difference between the transient character of Broadway, for example, where salaries are high to compensate for the temporary nature of employment, and the relatively more permanent character of the season of orchestras or permanent professional theatres. These at least make a commitment for a definite season, no matter how short.

The core of the performing arts—the actor, the musician, the dancer, the singer, the stagehand, the scene painter, the trucker, the press agent, and sometimes even the usher and the ticket taker—is made up of union members. Management in effect is an agent for the performer in collecting money, providing the stage, and creating the audience. Hence, there is a clear demand for mutual responsibility. A constant balance has to be struck between management's drive for quality at a reasonable cost and the union's aim of job security with fair pay for services rendered. If either fails, both suffer.

It is precisely for this reason that there is considerable hope in mechanisms through which management and the unions discuss their problems in a relaxed atmosphere, without the pressure of a strike deadline. To tell employees, when a contract is about to expire, how badly off the employer is has never been a persuasive management tactic. More candor and more contact on a year-round basis would help both sides anticipate issues and achieve greater understanding of their mutual problems.

Arts Management Training

The conduct of labor negotiations is only one of arts management's many preoccupations. There are daily crises relating to backstage and front-of-house operation that must be coped with; there are public relations to be maintained, everything from press releases to arranging opening night parties for subscribers. The general manager of an arts organization holds a position that has few counterparts in other fields. It is of great importance as these organizations proliferate that there be a comparable increase in the number of men and women equipped to supply high-grade managerial skills.

The American Symphony Orchestra League recognized this problem in 1952 when it launched a management training program that has been operating one week a year ever since. Over sixty persons now employed in managerial positions with orchestras and arts councils have attended the course. Recognizing that a one-week course could provide little more than orientation, the League moved on to offer an In-Service Management Training Program, aided by grants from the Avalon Foundation and the Martha Baird Rockefeller Fund for Music. Under these grants five young men have completed their year of training with leading orchestras and now serve as managers of substantial orchestras; two others are currently in training.

In 1961, the Ford Foundation launched a similar in-service program to train managers for arts organizations. In 1964, the third year of that program, twenty-four interns were provided with the opportunity to work for one year in an apprentice managerial capacity with outstanding nonprofit professional theatres, opera companies, and symphony orchestras.

Good as these programs may be, it must be recognized that arts administration cannot be left to improvement on such a modest scale, or to trial and error, or to the hope that somehow sufficient information will pass from one person to another. The steps that have been taken to train a new generation are welcome, but more effort, on a more formal basis, needs to be made—perhaps within the universities.

COOPERATION IN THE ARTS

The strength and efficiency of performing arts organizations rest on the ability of each one to handle its own problems. Expert assistance from without can, however, be of great value to the individual organization. There is an evident need for increasing communication in the performing arts both within and among the various fields. Not only is there a dearth of systematized information on the operations of performing arts organizations, there is still insufficient cooperation among them, despite the promise cooperation holds and despite the advances that have been made.

Arts Councils

The success of cooperative movements in health and welfare has led many community leaders to turn to the arts council idea as a means of stimulating practical cooperation among the arts organizations and focusing community attention on their activities, while at the same time preserving the artistic independence of each institution.

Most of the 100 community arts councils are organized as nonprofit, tax-exempt institutions.* Some accept memberships from individuals, others admit only organizations. Delegates from the member organizations serve on some councils' boards of directors, while other councils prefer to select their members from the community at large. Arts councils usually obtain their administrative funds by soliciting contributions and charging nominal dues. Some that conduct annual united fund-raising campaigns receive a share of the total raised.

There are hazards in the operation of an arts council, largely those of bureaucracy, but these can be avoided if the leadership has sufficient experience and high quality. Councils provide important services that are often missing or when available are needlessly duplicated by individual organizations: central clerical and promotional services for members, professional leadership for fund raising, publication of periodic calendars of events, advice in scheduling performances, and provision of management counseling services. Many councils have raised funds for community arts centers and are responsible for their operation. Approximately thirty councils include arts festivals in their programs.

The Winston-Salem Arts Council and the Saint Paul Council of Arts and Sciences have been in the vanguard of

* State arts councils are discussed in Chapter 7, and the work of the fourteen community arts councils that conduct united fund-raising campaigns is discussed more fully in Chapter 4.

the movement, and their work has set an example for other communities. One of the former's many successful projects has been its campaign to increase support for the Winston-Salem Symphony Orchestra. In the 1963–64 season, for example, the membership drive to fill a 2,000-seat auditorium produced 2,124 season memberships. The Saint Paul Council has recently completed a $3 million Arts and Science Center for its members and has steadily increased its united fund contributions. It has also been effective in promoting cooperative ventures among members. For example, both the Arts Center and the Science Museum, in cooperation with the Philharmonic Society, have given evening programs for students at the Philharmonic's Summer Music Camp. Informal luncheons scheduled by the Council director every two or three weeks for the professional directors of the six member organizations have been useful in fostering the cooperative spirit.

In 1960, individuals interested in the arts council movement formed a central clearinghouse for arts councils. Arts Councils of America (formerly Community Arts Councils, Inc.) issues a handbook and periodic bulletins to its members on fund-raising methods, arts calendars, festival promotions, and other cooperative arts projects. The organization also sponsors an annual conference for exchange of information and exposure to expert views on a wide range of artistic and management problems.

A Service Association for Each Art

The diversity of the various performing arts and the differences between the organizations within each field might create impossible complexities for a national "trade association" that attempts to serve all of them. But the need for service can be accomplished by strengthening existing organizations—like the American National Theatre and Academy, the American Symphony Orchestra League, the Central Opera Service, and the Theatre Communications Group—and establishing new ones as necessary.

The American Symphony Orchestra League was founded in 1942. Its purpose is to assist orchestras to strengthen their work, stabilize their financial base, expand their cultural services within their own communities, and reach toward higher artistic standards.

The League sponsors study and training projects for musicians, conductors, managers, and members of orchestral boards and women's associations. It holds an annual convention. It provides an advisory service to its individual members on many problems, including assistance in locating personnel. It publishes a newsletter and special reports on various aspects of orchestra work, including concert attendance, comparative finances, and statistics.

Working expenses for the League are financed largely from membership dues and contributions. In 1963–64, the amount came to approximately $86,000. Funds for special projects and activities are made available to the League by foundations, music organizations, and individuals, and totaled approximately $119,000 in the same year. In addition, the League receives almost $100,000 annually in contributed services. Expenditures for the operations of most other service organizations in the arts are small by comparison.

With the number of performing arts groups increasing all the time, with the strong desire for expansion in already established groups, more effective service organizations could be very useful in each of the performing arts. Given the stringent budgets of most arts groups, it must be assumed that they will need outside support. The institutions that would benefit the most from the strengthening of existing service organizations or the establishment of new ones are the least able to support them financially.

A NATIONAL CENTER FOR INFORMATION

In addition to the encouragement of community arts councils and national service organizations for the various arts, there is need for a national repository of information, a place to which inquiries about all the performing arts may be directed. Despite the diversity of problems confronting the various arts, it is also evident that there are many common problems as well, and that groups in each field can learn from the experience of the others and that the general public needs to know more about all of them.

First and foremost, a central institution would collect existing information about the operations of professional performing arts organizations and about the activities of all organizations in the arts. Its library should not duplicate existing collections, but complete bibliographies could be prepared on organization, management, and financing. There is also need to collate and analyze new material on a continuing basis in order to make it useful to the organizations and to the general public.

In addition, a bulletin is needed to set forth facts and figures about the activities of various groups as well as special articles about attendance, box office, financing, fund raising, facility construction, organization, and the like. The sponsorship of conferences to extend knowledge about the arts would also be valuable.

Finally, the center might undertake research projects

in problems of interest to any or all of the performing arts, although this function would perhaps be more wisely initiated as a second stage in the development of the center.

In all its programs this center would have to cooperate in the closest manner with the national service associations that already exist in order to eliminate duplication of effort. Certain activities would clearly be the responsibility of the service organizations. Technical advice to individual organizations and the operation of an employment service are examples of work it would not undertake.

In summary, the panel believes there is urgent need for an independent national information center that can assume an important and continuing role in the development of the performing arts and urges that every encouragement be given to its establishment.

9
The University and the Professional Performing Arts

The traditional role of the university in the arts has been to develop appreciation and understanding among its students. This role has greatly expanded in the years since World War II, and many universities now find themselves involved in areas of experience that are quite new to them. Some have become homes for professional arts groups and artists-in-residence; almost all have discovered that their responsibilities as artistic impresarios, offering more programs of higher caliber to their own and surrounding communities, have grown mightily. Still others are attempting to strengthen their arts and humanities programs in an effort to maintain a balance between them and the burgeoning teaching and research programs in the sciences and to contribute to a greater public appreciation of the arts.

Nor is this an end to the growth of the university's influence in our artistic life. Some colleges are now training professional performing artists, a responsibility that presents problems not only for the university but for everyone interested in the growth of the performing arts.

TRAINING PROFESSIONAL ARTISTS

As independent drama schools, art institutes, and music conservatories have declined in number, the universities with a generally broader base of public and private support have begun to assume increasing responsibility for training future performers.

The universities have become particularly involved with music. Although conservatories like Curtis, Juilliard, Manhattan, and Peabody still remain the primary source of professional training, the independent conservatory as the bastion of professional musical training has been under siege. Ideas of education have changed, costs have risen, and the universities and colleges have moved into the field. They have established schools of music that are virtually conservatories or have incorporated already existing conservatories within their structure.

Indiana University and the University of Southern California, with faculties that include many successful professional artists, exemplify this trend. There are others: Boston, Howard, and Northwestern universities; Mills College; the universities of Kansas, Illinois, and Michigan.

The Eastman School of Music and the Oberlin Conservatory of Music were precursors in this field, having been incorporated within university structures many years ago.

Training facilities for professional careers in the theatre are rudimentary compared to those for musicians. There are independent drama schools, several of excellent quality, such as the American Academy of Dramatic Arts and the Neighborhood Playhouse School of the Theatre in New York, the Goodman School of Drama in Chicago, and the Pasadena Playhouse in California, but there are few university drama departments of high standards. Among the universities and colleges offering training for professional careers, Yale University and the Carnegie Institute of Technology are outstanding. The Yale University School of Drama was established in 1955, but the university has offered training at the graduate level since the twenties. The department of drama in the College of Fine Arts at Carnegie Tech was established in 1914 and trains students at both an undergraduate and graduate level. Both Yale and Carnegie Tech number many successful professional actors, directors, designers, and stage technicians among their alumni.

But professional training in drama is available in too few places in this country, and where available, it is often offered only at the graduate level. Instead of a formal system of theatre education, most of our finest actors and directors have developed through a master-apprentice relationship, usually with an eminent theatrical figure. The result has been something of a patchwork. There are frequent complaints, for example, that while we have highly skilled naturalistic performers of contemporary drama, there is a dearth of professionals trained in the classics. No doubt some of this is due to the paucity of professional repertory opportunities and to Broadway's indifference to the great works of the past, but there is also a lack of thorough training at an early stage. Indeed, the High School of Performing Arts in New York, where talented teenage youngsters are given basic training in drama, music, or dance, might have counterparts in a dozen other great city school systems, provided adequate teachers could be found. Correcting the overall deficiency of training facilities in the theatre is one of the major challenges for the performing arts.

Although opportunities in dance education are more limited, sound professional academies of ballet and modern dance do exist. Like the conservatories, however, they are centered almost exclusively in the eastern part of the country. In the dance, training must begin in the subteens, and it must be of high competence if irreparable harm is not to be done to the novice.

At its 1964 conference the National Council of the Arts in Education expressed the view that dance should be given the status of an art, administratively and curricularly. Such courses as are presently offered are generally under the aegis of the physical education department, are available almost exclusively for women, and are intended primarily for teacher training or community dance work. The training is usually in modern dance rather than ballet.

There are some who feel that proper training cannot take place in the context of general education, and that university educators do not understand the single-minded concentration that must go into the training of the professional performer. They feel that private professional schools and conservatories are the only institutions capable of providing the environment and discipline that nurtures commitment to the arts. Sufficient evidence is by no means available to support these claims. *However, the panel believes schools and conservatories of recognized standards must not be allowed to weaken or disappear, as some have in recent decades. They must, instead, be strengthened, for they continue to produce the majority of solo artists and the ensemble musicians who man our finest musical institutions; from them come some of our best trained actors and virtually all our professional dancers.*

There is, indeed, some disagreement among educators over the assumption by a university or college of any responsibility for training professional performing artists. The question is whether highly specialized training in the techniques of these arts is a proper function of a university. To date there is no clearcut answer in practice or in stated policy. Some universities, Harvard and Princeton, for example, admit the performing arts only as extracurricular activities. A few, as noted above, have established professional schools on their campuses. Several have built what are probably the finest theatre buildings in the country. Most, however, have not yet formulated a firm policy. But pressures for professional training seem bound to grow, and an affirmative position will almost certainly be taken sooner or later. If a university is hospitable to specialized training in fields like medicine or engineering, it is only a question of time before specialized training in the performing arts will also be accepted as an appropriate role for institutions of higher education.

If a university or college does undertake this role, it must recognize the necessity of making appropriate adjustments in its institutional arrangements. At present admissions criteria emphasize academic attainments and have little relevance to creative ability in the arts. Admissions policies will have to be re-examined so that students with identifiable artistic potential may receive credit for performance courses and can be admitted even though they have not completed all the standard academic course requirements.

The universities and colleges will also have to develop flexibility in their curriculums and in scheduling classes to insure that students who wish to prepare themselves for performing careers are given the opportunity to concentrate single-mindedly on their art.

Teachers of the arts in universities have heretofore been primarily oriented toward art history and the training of musicologists, museum directors, historians, and teachers. Universities—and high schools—are beginning to attract successful performing artists who are also good teachers, regardless of their academic qualifications. Such faculty additions must be welcomed, for just as no university can contemplate establishing a medical school unless it has access to a hospital for internship and a staff of practitioners to teach, so no university should undertake professional training in the performing arts unless it is prepared to offer comparable facilities and staff.

Facilities might well be provided through professional organizations connected with the universities to which advanced students could be attached as apprentices. Opportunities with some orchestras are now informally provided for students. The Professional Theatre Program at the University of Michigan and the Theatre Group at UCLA provide apprenticeships for graduate students in drama, and the University of Minnesota has an arrangement with the Tyrone Guthrie Theatre through which graduate students are given similar opportunity to work in the theatre and gain credit toward graduate degrees. This type of cooperation between professional organizations and universities should be expanded and new forms of collaboration developed.

In summary, the panel believes that the universities will play an increasingly important role in the training of professional performing artists. Those universities that decide to assume a responsibility for professional training must be prepared to adjust their admissions policies and curricular requirements as necessary to meet the special needs of students of the performing arts, and they must attract the most highly qualified performing artists as teachers to their faculties.

ARTISTS-IN-RESIDENCE

A role of increasing importance for the college and university is to provide residence and sponsorship for performing artists and performing arts groups. The creative artists—painters, sculptors, writers, and composers—were the first to establish themselves in the university. Many contemporary composers are in residence on university campuses, and university and college teaching provides the principal economic security for many American painters and sculptors. Many American authors are writers-in-residence, with little responsibility for teaching; others are regular faculty members. Professional performing artists are less at home on our campuses than writers, perhaps because the performing artists need an organization with which to work. But there are many more of these groups—especially theatres and chamber music ensembles—on campuses today than was the case a few years ago.

Providing a home for the performing artist or group is as justifiable for a university as opening its laboratories to scientists for research. These artists can provide an opportunity for students to see and hear professional performances and can enhance the cultural climate of the campus. For performers, the principal advantages of university affiliation are institutional stability and financial security, both of which are difficult to acquire without aid.

RESEARCH AND EXPERIMENTATION

Research and experimentation in the performing arts are an important new role for the university. No other institution in our society is so well fitted to provide the necessary resources, and the work that has been done indicates there are exciting possibilities for the development of new techniques and forms in the arts. Experiments in electronic music and in the development of new staging and lighting techniques already have been launched and could well be expanded. Research into the conditions under which performers and artistic talent best flourish could be undertaken. Studies might usefully be made of many facets of the live, recorded, and televised presentations of the arts: the differences between the forms of presentation, the techniques of presentation, the response by the viewer to each, the effect of the electronic media on the live arts, and so forth. Indeed, research is needed in all the performing arts just to find out what research is needed.

THE UNIVERSITY AS IMPRESARIO

Universities and colleges have for many years sponsored performances on their campuses. Nearly all of them have some concert series, varying from modest programs that include only a few soloists to very large programs that sponsor appearances by the finest dance groups, orchestras, and opera and theatre companies. The University of Michigan Musical Society program is a representative example of the expansion that has occurred in recent years. In 1953–54, the Society's budget was $129,557 and included twenty-six programs. In 1963–64, its estimated budget was $275,000 and included forty-one programs. Types of presentations have expanded, too. In many universities the concert bureau has assumed the stature of a division or department within the institution. Programs are financed in a variety of ways—through subscriptions, general admissions, student activities fees, university grants, or combinations of these.

The expansion of the university's role as impresario offers the encouraging prospect of more employment for professional artists and increased availability of cultural opportunities for greater numbers of people. University concert bureaus are generally free from commitment to the star system and have provided young, relatively unknown artists with opportunities to establish their reputations. Indeed, without them the modern dance could not exist at all in this country. In many parts of the country the university is the only agency capable of organizing programs of high quality in all the arts. In this respect it provides a public service for which, as a public institution, it is uniquely qualified.

THE UNIVERSITY AND THE COMMUNITY

Performing arts organizations located on campus and performances by visiting groups provide cultural opportunities for the communities in which the universities are located as well as for the students and faculty. This community service role has grown in recent years, and state universities have been especially concerned with it as a proper function of a tax-supported institution. In large cities the university's role of service to the community is less important than in smaller communities where the university or college becomes the cultural hub for the surrounding area. Changing population patterns in the United States account in part for the educational institution's growing importance in this respect. As populations expand in the undefinable areas of exurbia, enormous numbers of people find themselves living in communities with no real centers. Without jeopardizing its primary obligation to the students, a university can provide a cultural focus that would otherwise be lacking in these areas.

It is important that conscientious and continuing efforts be made to insure that community planning and educational planning of performing arts programs are coordinated. Cooperation might be facilitated by university membership on local arts councils.

DEVELOPING PUBLIC INTEREST IN THE PERFORMING ARTS

Perhaps the most important role of the university and the liberal arts college is, and has traditionally been, development of an appreciation and understanding of the arts as part of a broad general education in the humanities. Many educators still believe this is the university's only legitimate function in the arts.

Responsiveness to the performing arts is created through knowledge and attendance, and educational institutions have consequently had an enormous influence on the development of discerning audiences. An important factor in the growing interest in the arts in America has been the expanding audience coming from the increasingly higher proportion of the population with college degrees.

But the humanities generally are at a disadvantage compared to the physical sciences in our universities, and the imbalance appears to be growing. Special aid from the federal government is available for science programs in universities. This in turn attracts matching funds from other sources, putting the humanities at a still further disadvantage. This long-range trend in American education can only have an adverse effect on audience development for the arts. *The panel believes there is urgent need to redress the existing imbalance in the financial support of the physical sciences and that of the arts and humanities in universities.*

There are many techniques available for achieving this balance. They range from the creation of new professional training schools to the expansion of courses in the appreciation of the arts. All universities cannot and should not attempt all of these things. Each will have to consider the needs of its students and community in determining what it should undertake. But the university is one of the natural homes for the arts, and it should be encouraged to extend the range of its hospitality in the years to come.

10
Building Greater Appreciation

A basic problem for the performing arts is to create an environment favorable to their growth. It is not enough for our country to have artists of high quality. It is not enough to have strong performing arts institutions—opera companies, repertory theatres, symphony orchestras, choral and chamber music groups, dance companies. There must also be a sizable public prepared through education, both formal and informal, to receive aesthetic pleasure from their efforts and eager to join in the attempt to enhance the nation's cultural life. Without a public of this kind, the artist has no one with whom to communicate, arts institutions operate in a vacuum, and there cannot be growth and liveliness in our culture.

Does such an audience exist today? If not, is it likely to develop in the near future? These questions are impossible to answer with statistical accuracy. We simply do not know who composes the public for art, nor its exact size, nor the degree of its commitment, nor the factors that have created the interest in the arts that now exists in our society. There is, to be sure, evidence both empirical and intuitive to indicate that there has been an appreciable increase in the audience for the arts over the last decade. But against this must be set a strong, countervailing impression, equally unprovable statistically, that the arts in general, and the performing arts in particular, do not yet have deep or strong roots in the lives of the majority of our people.

As a nation we have traditionally possessed no great thirst for music, dance, drama; if anything we have inherited a suspicion that the practice of these arts is unmanly and superfluous and that support of them is of no vital importance to our national well-being. So long as ballet dancing or piano playing is considered long-haired or "sissy" and painters and poets something apart, the climate will remain unsuitable for the development of appreciation. We are now in a transitional stage in which these attitudes are changing. A further change in the climate will depend on the attitudes of community leaders in all walks of life—public officials, businessmen, the press, labor, the clergy, and, perhaps most of all, educators.

EDUCATION

The creation of a propitious environment for the arts depends primarily upon the education of a people. Any significant increase in demand for the performing arts will derive only from a citizenry that has come to love them and to depend on them. Furthermore, the pursuit of excellence in the arts, without which their expansion is meaningless, grows only from a general public recognition of what constitutes high quality. Mediocrity is the menace that lies inherent in egalitarianism. The only weapon that can be used to combat it is education; and again, not a mediocre education but one that produces an appreciation of form and a basic concern for the things of the mind and spirit.

Obviously this cannot be accomplished quickly. But if it is to be accomplished at all, there are steps to be taken now and in the years immediately ahead. The habit of attendance is based on a strong sense of need—and without a sense of urgent necessity on the part of the people, the performing arts will always remain peripheral, exotic, and without any true significance. Therefore, the habit must be acquired young; it is probably not too soon to begin at six. After all, at that age boys are learning how to play baseball. Music and dancing and play-acting come naturally to children at that age. This can easily be translated into the pleasures of seeing and hearing others perform.

The role of the family at this stage cannot be overemphasized. If it is not interested in the arts, is not willing to offer youngsters at least an occasional opportunity to satisfy their curiosity about what goes on inside the theatre or recital hall or opera house, then no formal effort at cultural education is likely to be very successful. A family climate that reinforces the school's efforts to introduce the child to the pleasures of the performing arts is of inestimable underlying importance in enlarging the audiences of the future.

For the school to make sure that a child attends a concert, a play, or a dance recital once a year for ten years will neither allow the child to acquire a habit nor create a sense of necessity about art. These pleasures will remain something to take or leave, and the chances are on the side of the latter. But to provide live performances for young people with sufficient frequency, quality, and range to establish a lifelong habit is generally impossible within the context of American education at the present time. Is there any chance that this context can be changed? And if so, how?

The Schools

While the performing arts have traditionally been a part of the school curriculum, the development of selective performing groups—bands, orchestras, and choruses—representing a relatively small segment of the total school population, has generally been stressed. Only minor attention has been given to cultivating the artistic tastes of the large mass of students not engaged in performing organizations. Many school musical and dramatic groups achieve a high level of technical proficiency, but they can be justly criticized for devoting too much time and effort to music and drama that is trivial and inconsequential. The objective often seems to be solely to entertain rather than to educate.

The self-contained classroom prevailing in elementary

schools for several decades has worked against the development of an effective program of instruction in the arts. We need more and better trained teachers in the arts, particularly at the elementary school level. School administrators need to be made more aware of the place of the arts in a balanced curriculum and the necessity for providing not only adequate time during the school day but also the materials and equipment needed for an arts program. Greater experimentation with newly developed teaching aids and materials should be sought. School officials should be encouraged to make full use of the artistic resources of the community, both professional and amateur, in stimulating and enriching the education program in the arts.

New York, which naturally has the largest public school population of any city in the country and also the richest performing arts resources on which to draw, has tackled the problem of exposing its younger citizens to art through the Bureau of Audio-Visual Instruction of the Board of Education. It serves as both sponsor and clearinghouse for a multitude of programs, ranging from a children's Saturday theatre to in-service training programs in theatre and opera appreciation for its teachers. It arranges for performances in the schools by professional troupes and negotiates with Broadway and other concert and theatrical managements for cut-rate tickets for students.

While other cities may not have comparable resources to tap, their school boards might, more frequently than they do, establish "audio-visual bureaus" or their equivalents to assume responsibility for this part of children's education. The American school, in general, should show greater imagination, initiative, and responsibility than it has in bringing art to the school and the child to art.

Independent Agencies

Arts organizations and independent agencies are also helping build greater appreciation among children of school age and might well be aided in expanding their work. An analysis of a questionnaire recently answered by some 250 Columbia Broadcasting System station managers reveals that in cities of under 50,000, educational institutions are considered to have made the greatest contribution to audience development, but in cities of over 50,000, it is performing arts organizations themselves—including arts councils and independent agencies like Young Audiences—that are generally credited with making the greatest contribution.

Young Audiences is an outstanding example of what can be done on independent initiative. Utilizing some six hundred professional artists in all parts of the country, it has in fourteen years brought chamber music into public, private, and parochial schools to reach a total audience of some fifteen million children. It now presents over five thousand concerts in some 325 communities during the school year. Recently this national, nonprofit organization has expanded its activity to include excerpts from opera. Over two dozen television performances have been presented during the past five years, several of which have been bought by National Educational Television. Young Audiences' current expenses are in the neighborhood of $100,000 a year. Each school pays about $115 for a concert plus minimum travel expenses, although many pay considerably less as a result of fund-raising efforts by their local chapters. Much is being accomplished by skilled, dedicated leadership with a comparatively small outlay of funds.

In California, a group called Junior Programs, sponsored by a consortium of universities, each of whose drama departments guarantees a production, offers six to ten productions annually to consistently sold-out houses. Other higher education institutions, such as the University of Denver, have a notable record of work with young audiences.

In Chicago, the James C. Petrillo Foundation was established in 1961 by the Chicago Federation of Musicians. Its funds are used to present concerts by its members in the city's elementary schools. Woodwind quintets, string quartets, and brass and percussion ensembles offer programs featuring such composers as Ives, Prokofiev, and Hindemith; there are also demonstrations of individual instruments and question-and-answer sessions. The program costs the Chicago Federation $25,000 annually; it is a rare and welcome example of aid to the arts offered by one of their own unions.

The worldwide Jeunesses Musicales movement was established in 1940 in France and Belgium, for the purpose of making good music a part of youthful lives, and it has spread to Italy, Denmark, and Canada. In France, where it receives some government support, its membership comprises 250,000 young people in every part of the country. They attend a wide variety of theatre, concert, opera, and ballet performances at prices far below the box office, averaging about $.84 per performance. In May of 1964, the organization of Jeunesses Musicales in the United States was announced. It plans to set up local chapters, principally at colleges throughout the country, and will function without government support. Each chapter will sponsor low-price concerts by touring artists. At the moment the U.S. organization is young and fragile, but it, or something like it, could become an important instrument in making the arts available to an age group that cannot afford regular ticket prices.

Arts Organizations

In recent years performing arts organizations themselves have assumed greater responsibility for building appreciation of their arts among youth. Observing what has been done in Europe, some have established children's matinees, other youth events, and special student ticket prices. The Comédie Française, for instance, gives Thursday and Sunday matinees for students at prices from $.33 to $1.15, and the Swedish Riksteater sets aside fifty to one hundred seats for students at regular performances priced between $.59 and $.97.

As yet, nothing has been created in this country to compare with the Children's Theatres and Theatres for Young Spectators in the Soviet Union. In Moscow and Leningrad—and in other cities too—one or more thousand-seat houses have been set aside for constant and exclusive use by companies of top professionals who perform eight to ten times weekly for audiences that range in age from six to eighteen. Offering repertories of classics and new plays written especially for youngsters, they work in close conjunction with the schools, select works that will be appropriate for various age levels, and provide drama for an annual audience that numbers approximately half a million in each of the two major cities.

In the United States, the pioneers in providing programs for youth have been the music organizations. Some orchestras, like the Baltimore Symphony, present concerts in school auditoriums on school time as an integral part of the instructional program. Many other orchestras have young people's concerts as part of their regular services. In fact, it is safe to say, there is hardly a symphony orchestra in the country that does not make a considerable effort to get children interested in music.

In introducing young people to opera, the Metropolitan has made a comparable contribution through an annual series of seven student matinees. These have been sponsored since 1937 by the Metropolitan Opera Guild, and over the years almost half a million student tickets have been dispensed. The San Francisco Opera Guild finances four student matinees annually. For the Spring Opera season at popular prices, the audience is young; but according to Kurt Adler, general manager of the San Francisco Opera, "they are devotees of opera, and those who can afford it graduate to the fall season." At the Chicago Lyric Opera, a single student matinee was underwritten for the first time in 1963 by the Junior Chamber of Commerce, and the number was increased to two in 1964. This is a happy augury even though the 3,600-seat opera house only accommodates a tiny fraction of Chicago's hundreds of thousands of students.

Although the New York City Ballet has been forced to cancel its performances for underprivileged children because of lack of funds, it has still been able to offer between forty and fifty lecture-demonstrations annually in the city schools.

Turning to theatre, one notes that there are a few small troupes especially designed to play for children. There are also examples of theatres that have shouldered the task of building youth audiences. The Phoenix Theatre in New York between 1960 and 1962 took an itinerant company offering a program of excerpts from the classical drama to 242 schools, but was forced to stop for lack of funds. By arrangement with the Bureau of Audio-Visual Instruction, it played *Hamlet* in 1961 to more than 100,000 students in its own theatre and for three years conducted a teacher training program in theatre appreciation. In 1963, it leased a second 1,600-seat house in downtown Manhattan, priced tickets at $1.50, and presented two full productions at a series of special performances for students. The New York Shakespeare Festival also has taken free Shakespeare to the schools, playing before 56,000 students during the fall of 1963. In the late spring of 1964, 107,000 students went from far and near to Stratford, Connecticut, and paid $2 each to see performances of the American Shakespeare Festival Theatre's repertory, the sixth year this program had been undertaken. In 1965, the student program will be expanded from nine to twelve weeks as part of its twenty-seven-week season.

While these examples of activity by the schools, by independent agencies, and by the arts organizations themselves are heartening, it must be candidly admitted that they are but a fraction of what will have to be provided if the education of young people in the live performing arts is to be measurably broadened in our lifetime. The proportions of the task are of such magnitude as to give us all pause. Moreover, these same young people grow to become tomorrow's taxpayers and legislators, mayors and governors, corporation and foundation executives, and labor and civic leaders. If the arts are to receive any substantial increase in support from any of these sources, it will be because we have leaders who are educated to an appreciation of art's value to the community.

The effective exposure of young people to the arts is as much a civic responsibility as programs in health and welfare.

Although the panel recognizes that the initiative for an expanded educational effort in the arts will generally come from individuals, success in the measure necessary will require the combined backing of the family and the school system. Also important are the encouragement of private organizations, local and state arts councils, and the cooperation of local governments and the federal Office of Education.

AVAILABILITY OF PERFORMANCES

For adults, too, the actual presence of the performing arts is essential to audience development. The ready availability of music in Germany, Austria, and Italy, of drama and ballet in Russia, has no counterpart today in America. For the vast majority of Americans, even those dwelling in cities, a live professional performance of a play, an opera, a symphony, or a ballet is an altogether uncommon experience. Samuel R. Rosenbaum, trustee of the Recording Industries Music Performance Trust Funds, estimates that the number of different persons who make up the present paying audiences for the live professional performing arts does not exceed 1 percent of the population.

The New Mobility

Many more resident professional performing arts organizations are needed in communities throughout the country, but if the arts are to be made as widely available as is desirable, the panel emphasizes the necessity of increasing the mobility of the performing arts by new means and on a new scale. To be sure, the Metropolitan Opera tours, as does the New York City Ballet, and the major symphony orchestras do some touring. Sol Hurok sends foreign dance and theatre companies across the country, and various concert managers arrange tours of soloists, but these do not reach enough cities with regularity. The theatrical road is thorny and ill-marked.

All of these are examples of "the road" as it is traditionally understood. What is needed is a new, broader concept of touring, of increased mobility. Established organizations touring within a state under the sponsorship of a state arts council is a recent development. Another new kind of touring is that undertaken within a single metropolitan area, bringing theatre or music to people who are remote psychologically rather than physically from the cultural center of things. So is touring by a regional company, its settings and equipment specifically designed for a homeless life. So is touring by a company set up to appeal to a specific kind of audience—children, workers, the institutionalized.

Some examples: The New York State Council on the Arts has sponsored hundreds of performances of plays, concerts, opera, and dance recitals in cities throughout the state during the first four years of its operation. When *Hamlet,* for instance, played towns like Middletown and Oneonta, it was the first live professional theatre performance since Texas Guinan appeared there in the twenties. It may have been partly curiosity that moved them, but people filled the local halls to overflowing.

A more dramatic example of the new mobility is provided by the summer tours of the New York Shakespeare Festival into the five boroughs of New York City. In the summer of 1964, with the cooperation of the City, it took a mobile unit playing *A Midsummer Night's Dream* to thirty-four locations, giving fifty-four performances. Describing the opening night in Harlem, Howard Taubman, drama critic of *The New York Times,* reported: "The 1,600 seats provided by the festival's rolling theatre were occupied by a lot more than 1,600 persons. The audience included a host of small fry, and in many cases they sat two in a seat. In addition, there were many babies on laps and in arms, since Harlem mothers don't always have the money to hire sitters. One or two of the smallest were hitting the bottle and several were asleep, but there was virtually no crying. The older children could not have been more attentive if they had been sitting through a mystery or a Western."

Something like the Swedish Riksteater may be needed in America. For thirty years this national touring theatre has sent performers to some 350 remote towns—some within the Arctic Circle—not once but eight or ten times a year. Indeed, all told the Riksteater sells some half a million tickets a year and gives close to two thousand performances. After a French government survey in 1945 disclosed that no more people were attending the theatre in that year than had attended in 1789, the government started a program to establish theatre companies in eight cities outside Paris. These *centres dramatiques* now perform regularly in their surrounding areas as well as in the cities where they are based. In the United States, far wider circulation of all types of performing arts groups is needed.

Increased mobility of the arts can be accomplished in a number of ways: through a proliferation of state arts councils organized and financed to assist groups to tour (presuming, of course, that companies are available to them for touring); through arrangements by permanent professional theatres and music and dance organizations to tour in their surrounding areas; and through utilization of university extension facilities to provide tours by professional groups throughout a state or region. (Again, this presupposes the existence of groups associated with universities.)

Scheduling

To attract new audiences requires much more imaginative planning and scheduling of performances than now exists. A leaf might be taken from the book of Jean Vilar, who established the Théâtre National Populaire in Paris in 1951. Not in any sense a "labor theatre," his aim was to create a theatre for the workingman. He made it one of the most successful theatres in the country, drawing today all levels of the entire theatregoing public.

Recognizing that theatre was entirely outside the experience of a great segment of the French public, Vilar set out to transform not the man but the theatre. He had faith in the worker's response to good theatre, and he started his own revolution. He established a theatre with prices suited to the worker's purse, changed the hours of performance to fit the working day, and did away with the traditions and encumbrances of theatregoing that tended to make it a forbidding experience. There were inexpensive meals conveniently available at the theatre and special transportation was provided. He put out a newspaper that generated interest in the works to be played. He provided resumes of each play as well as illustrated paperbacks of the work itself. He went to the workers of Paris and appealed directly for support for his idea. Today, many of his ideas are being adopted in other parts of France.

Mass Media

Television, radio, and recordings offer the technical means to provide virtually every American with the possibility of witnessing—albeit remotely—performances of high quality. There is no possibility now for live performances of similar quality to reach this mass audience. Hence, the media have a unique opportunity to fill a gap that is likely to exist indefinitely.

Recordings and radio have made a substantial contribution to the growth of concert audiences and continue to do so. In recent years FM radio stations, many of them programing many hours of good music each day, have exerted a strong influence on the nation's musical tastes. Recordings, too, have done much to bring music and, to some extent, drama to a wider audience and to raise performance standards.

With few exceptions, radio stations and record companies in this country operate under commercial auspices, limiting the variety of programing and the encouragement of new and unfamiliar music and drama. A scattering of nonprofit ventures in radio and recording has demonstrated the possibility of filling these gaps and deserves to be strengthened and supported by the public.

Television's contribution to building audiences for the live performing arts is more difficult to assess. Technically it offers unrivaled possibilities of reaching and developing a vast audience. But the economics of commercial television have compelled it to become heavily dependent on the attention of an already existing mass audience, and many programs of value to the serious performing arts have disappeared in recent years. There is no indication that the trend will be reversed in the foreseeable future.

Attempts to resolve the problem through pay or subscription television are still in the experimental stages. Furthermore, the techniques of production need considerable advancement before consistent quality presentation of the arts is achieved. In any case, it has not been established that the viewer of a television program transfers that experience into a desire for the live performance. Indeed, it may be contended that the live arts and the electronically transmitted arts are two quite separate forms. *This panel, however, believes the importance of the electronic media cannot be overstressed in increasing the availability of the performing arts of high quality and in creating new audiences and even new works for them. In the view of this panel, the commercial television industry has a definite responsibility to improve its methods of presentation and programing in the performing arts.*

Educational television, not being bound by the same requirements as commercial television, has potentially greater flexibility in programing material relating to the performing arts. It can encourage appreciation of fine drama and music; familiarize the audience with the complexities of technique in performance; increase appreciation of the modern and classical repertory through reiterated hearing; and illuminate matters of form and content through critical discussions.

But educational television generally has not done these things well enough or often enough. It lacks funds for the elaborate productions sometimes necessary for the successful television presentation of performing arts. In some cities it has been unable to reach agreement with performer unions and thus is barred from competing with the cultural presentations of commercial channels. It has not, in general, attracted top-quality television production talent capable of presenting the performing arts in a lively and imaginative style suited to the medium. Most serious of all, it is still debating its proper function: Should it be primarily a teaching service offering in-school services and adult education services? Or should it be a general cultural medium, offering, like the British Broadcasting Corporation radio's Third Programme, a quality of entertainment and information not elsewhere available in the mass media and deliberately serving the needs of a minority? When it surmounts these hurdles, when it decides what it is and what it wants to be, *the panel believes educational television has a great opportunity to make a significant contribution to the arts. The panel urges the community to provide the support necessary to exploit this opportunity vigorously.*

ART CRITICISM

The role of the critic in maintaining standards, weeding out the second- and third-rate, and casting a spotlight of approval upon the best is important in building greater appreciation. Save in a handful of major cities, newspaper criticism of musical, theatrical, and dance events is the responsibility of journalists with no specialized knowledge of the field. As artistic activity proliferates, there will be increasing need for the press to improve the quality of its critical comment. For smaller communities it might be feasible to have "circuit-riding" critics serving several newspapers.

An awareness of the inadequacy of current critical standards and a concern for excellence in art criticism is reflected in the recent interest displayed by both the Rockefeller and Ford foundations in helping to improve the standards of newspaper criticism and cultural reporting. The critics workshops of the American Symphony Orchestra League, which led to the formation of the Music Critics Association, were given support by the Rockefeller Foundation from 1956 to 1960. Beginning in 1964, it is supporting a four-year program at the University of Southern California to provide training and experience for both practicing and neophyte critics. In 1964, the Ford Foundation announced grants to eleven established art critics for travel, observation, and study; five of these were performing arts critics—three of drama, two of music. Well-informed but sympathetic criticism of the arts can do much to deepen audience awareness and encourage greater appreciation, as well as improve the art itself.

PROMOTION OF THE ARTS

Even with an educated public and performances readily available, the arts need promotion. In a country where public relations, publicity, advertising, and other promotional skills have been elevated to near-sciences, the performing arts have made little effective use of these devices. Lack of funds has been one reason for this. Not infrequently, however, performing arts organizations have seemed to feel that their mere existence would of itself attract an audience. In a competitive society this is not enough. Audience development can be substantially helped by the services of good and experienced public relations counsel and press agents.

It is sometimes asked why the press carries radio and television program listings daily at no charge to the media, while producers of concerts, dance recitals, and plays must regularly buy space at considerable cost—about $500 a week minimum for a New York theatre—in order even to be mentioned. The answer seems to be that the former are regarded as a public service because there is a large public to be served; the latter, having negligible readership interest, are penalized by many newspapers. This inequity can be remedied by a simple listing of events—at relatively small cost to newspapers, and to the considerable benefit of the arts.

Managements concerned with the problem of audience development might well ascertain whether the most convenient means of ticket distribution and sales are being employed; whether in large urban areas the suburban patron is being adequately served; whether parking and transportation facilities can be improved; whether special sales techniques—subscriptions, benefits, credit arrangements, group sales for special performances—are being utilized satisfactorily.

In connection with group sales it may be asked whether performing arts organizations are really trying to reach organized audience groups that exist or could be developed. One example is labor unions. The International Ladies Garment Workers Union has organized theatre parties and subsidized reduced-rate tickets for its members; it has contributed substantially to a series of concerts of the American Symphony Orchestra of New York and sold reduced-rate tickets for it to ILGWU members and their families. By and large, however, the limitless possibilities for union cooperation in audience development are all but unexplored.

A barrier to the creation of new audiences from the labor force is lack of interest. Yet, not many years ago unions had few general or political education programs, few ambitious health programs. The unions since have made immense strides in these and many other areas of concern to the lives of their members. It is reasonable to assume that with encouragement they will recognize the value of the arts as well.

The first AFL-CIO National Conference on Community Services in 1963 was devoted to an exploration of "The Shorter Work Week and the Constructive Use of Leisure Time." It was an initial step in labor's assumption of responsibility in this important area. Following that meeting, several regional conferences were held. Discussion guides aimed at illuminating the place of the arts in utilizing free time have gone out from New York to locals across the country. Field officers have been encouraged to make inventories of the cultural activities that already exist in their various communities.

In addition, articles on the arts might be included in union journals, and lectures on the arts could be included in union education programs, with selected speakers—writers, actors, directors—from Broadway, the films, and television, who would lend excitement to developing interest in the performing arts. The expense would not be overwhelming; the effect could be great.

A particularly promising road for the unions is arranging for the bloc-purchase of seats for a wide range of performances, as the ILGWU is doing. As regional theatres proliferate, as symphony orchestras extend their activities, and as opera travels more extensively, new opportunities for exposure arise. Doubtless, reduced-rate tickets could be provided by theatres looking for larger and steadier future audiences. Successful experiments along these lines have already been launched at the Tyrone Guthrie Theatre in Minneapolis and on occasion at Lincoln Center.

The unions are used here as an illustration of the

actions that can be taken by any "organized audience group" to increase appreciation for the arts. Labor has especially dramatic possibilities because of its size, but no less important are women's and men's organizations and voluntary associations of all kinds, so abundant in this country.

AMATEUR ACTIVITY

The extent to which amateur activity in the performing arts strengthens audiences for professional performances is a question on which opinions are deeply divided. Elmer Rice has estimated that the annual attendance at amateur theatrical performances is fifty million, which he believed to be probably ten times the attendance at professional performances. These spectacular figures do not apparently reflect any encouragement of professional growth; indeed, while amateur activity in the theatre and in some of the other performing arts has increased markedly, professional activity has decreased almost as markedly.

Amateurism may fail as an audience builder for professional performance in a number of ways. Inexperienced audiences, whose only exposure to the living theatre is through amateur dramatics of less than first-rate quality, sometimes compare it to the superior quality of television and motion pictures and conclude that the difference is in the media rather than in the level of acting. Robert Porterfield, director of Virginia's Barter Theatre, reports that at a particularly inept amateur performance he once heard a woman sitting in front of him say at its conclusion: "If this is theatre, let me stay home or go to the movies!"

Again, amateur and community groups occasionally

are antagonistic to professional drama—and vice versa—since both compete for box office and financial support. They also become rivals for the use of limited auditorium facilities.

Amateur antipathy toward the professional is frequently and regrettably inculcated on the university campus by educators whose principal interest seems to be in directing their students away from professional work and into educational or community work. While this is in part dictated by a realistic appraisal of the limited professional employment possibilities, it is frequently a reflection of the teacher's own bias against professionalism.

On the other hand, amateurism can be an ally of successful professional performance. Although it is more frequently a source of enjoyment for its participants than a contribution to the serious advancement of these arts, it can create a climate of appreciation essential to audience development. The individual who finds a personal commitment beyond his own satisfaction in playing in a string quartet at home with friends, or with a community orchestra, or in performing on the boards of the local little theatre, surely gains an increased understanding of the crafts involved.

The arts may have something to learn from sports. The community orchestras, for example, need guidance to improve standards. In baseball, leading professionals hold clinics for the amateurs—something that professional performing artists too rarely do. Further, since community orchestras serve to some extent as "farm teams" for the metropolitan and major orchestras, it is to their advantage for performance standards to rise. The analogy can be continued. Neither participation in sports, such as amateur golf and sandlot baseball, nor mass viewing of the professional variety, has led to the deterioration of quality in the professional game. On the contrary, they appear to have led to higher standards of professional performance and greater and more informed popular appreciation. A clear distinction between professional and amateur quality and standards has been maintained, a distinction that should be equally possible in the field of the arts.

So long as neither professional nor amateur confuses the two areas of expression and both retain a perspective toward excellence, the relationship between them can be lively and constructive. The panel believes that thriving amateurism can play a major role in creating audiences for high-quality professional performance and that amateur interests in the arts should be encouraged in every possible way.

11
The Challenge of the Performing Arts

This study of the performing arts is made with the conviction that the arts are one of the central elements of a good society, an essential of a full life for the many, not a luxury for the few. This conviction is shared by growing numbers of Americans, with the result that the arts are being given a far larger mission than they have been commonly accorded in the past.

Few can take issue with the objective of making the arts available to everyone who wishes to enjoy them. But an important cautionary note must be added if the actions discussed in this report are to be meaningful. We must never allow the central focus on quality to weaken or shift. Popularization in any realm often leads to a reduction of standards. In our effort to broaden the audience base, we must not be led to accept imitation as a substitute for creation, mediocrity as a stand-in for excellence. Democratization carries with it a peril for the arts, even as it does for education. There are no guarantees against the dilution of standards that often accompanies an expanding public, but a constant critical awareness of the danger can do much to prevent its consequences.

We can never expect to fill our concert halls, our theatres, our opera houses—the ones we now have and the ones we shall build—unless men and women and young people experience within their walls some new perception of man and the meaning of his life. We cannot hope to hold the audiences we now possess or gain new audiences without drama that is moving and exciting, music that stirs and grips the listener, and dance that creates true enjoyment. We may talk ad infinitum of box office prices and subscription campaigns, press agentry and public relations, classes and seminars and critics; the only thing that will draw and hold audiences, present and future, is a world of the performing arts that is vital, beautiful, and relevant—in classical as well as contemporary forms.

Organizations sponsoring and presenting the live professional performing arts have a special custodianship of high quality. Those that provide inspiring examples of excellence must be maintained, those that have yet to attain highest quality must strive continuously to improve their performance.

It is a bold venture to envisage a great enlargement of the mission of the performing arts—opera, instrumental and choral music, the dance, and theatre—when all of them are in deep economic difficulties in carrying out their present programs. However, the basic resources, human and material, for the full development of the arts do exist in the United States. The problem is to mobilize them and to use them effectively for the pleasure of the many. The panel is under no illusion that this can be accomplished easily or speedily; this report bristles with difficult problems to which there are no easy answers. But these problems can be solved by a nation that has already accomplished so much in the political, social, and economic realms. In the middle of the twentieth century the full development of our potential in the arts in general and in the performing arts in particular presents a challenge to the restless American spirit that will call upon its reserves of strength, imagination, and capacity to innovate. We believe the challenge is worthy of the nation and that the nation is equal to the challenge.

Notes and Sources

Chapter 1 The Arts in America

Page 2: The Eric Larrabee quotation as edited by him is originally from a report prepared for the National Cultural Center, now the John F. Kennedy Center for the Performing Arts, in October 1960, by G. A. Brakeley & Co., Inc., New York, p. 1. (Mimeographed.)

Page 2: Quotations from *The American* are from *Four Selected Novels of Henry James,* Grosset & Dunlap, New York, 1946, p. 52.

Page 4: The quotation is from the text of President Kennedy's address at Amherst College, October 26, 1963, as it appeared in *The New York Times* the following day.

Page 7: The Crawford H. Greenewalt quotation is from a speech at the Society of Chemical Industry, New York City, September 24, 1963.

Page 7: Thomas J. Watson's statement was made in an address to the American Council on Education, Washington, D.C., October 3, 1963.

Page 8: The quotation from the Henry Street Settlement was contained in a letter dated May 29, 1964.

Chapter 2 The Performing Arts—Today and Tomorrow

Page 13: The general information about the arts is given in 1963–64 figures unless noted otherwise. It is in part the result of Special Studies staff calculations based on the following sources: American Symphony Orchestra League; *Opera News* and Central Opera Service; Samuel French, Inc., and *Variety;* Richard Schickel, "Dance in America," a paper prepared for this study in 1964; Arnold Mitchell, *Marketing the Arts,* Stanford Research Institute, Menlo Park, California, 1962; and *Economic Conditions in the Performing Arts,* Hearings before the Select Subcommittee on Education of the House Committee on Education and Labor, 87th Cong., 1st and 2nd Sess., November 1961–February 1962.

Page 17: The hearings are reprinted in *Economic Conditions in the Performing Arts, ibid.*

Page 20: The general information and statistics about symphony orchestras throughout the report were obtained from the American Symphony Orchestra League and from papers prepared for this study. Specific information about individual orchestras was obtained from each directly. Unless indicated otherwise data is for 1963–64.

Page 24: The Herbert Graf statement is from his book *Producing Opera for America,* Atlantis Books, Zurich and New York, 1961, pp. 92–96.

Page 24: The information about choral music throughout the report is from a paper prepared for this study.

Page 26: The information about chamber music throughout the report is from a paper prepared for this study and from Harold Spivacke, chief, Music Division, Library of Congress.

Page 27: General information about opera throughout the report is from a paper prepared for this study. General statistics are from reports of the Central Opera Service and *Opera News* surveys. Information about individual opera companies was obtained from each directly. Unless indicated otherwise data is for 1963–64.

Page 33: The general information and statistics about theatre throughout the report are from several sources and in part are based on staff calculations. Unless indicated otherwise data is for 1963–64. The primary sources of information were Actors' Equity Association, American National Theatre and Academy, *Variety,* and several papers prepared for this study. Information on individual theatres was obtained from each directly by correspondence and questionnaire.

Page 41: The statement on outdoor dramas was derived from George McCalmon and Christian H. Moe, "Creating Historical Drama: A Guide for the Community and the Interested Individual," University of Southern Illinois, unpublished manuscript.

Page 42: The Walter Kerr quotation is from the *New York Herald Tribune,* August 30, 1964.

Page 43: General statistics on the dance throughout the report are from *Economic Conditions in the Performing Arts, op. cit.,* and from papers prepared for this study. Data about individual companies was obtained from each directly by correspondence and questionnaire.

Page 50: The cost estimates were based on consultations with experts in the performing arts and on staff analyses of financial information obtained directly from individual organizations and from the American Symphony Orchestra League.

Chapter 3 Box Office and Other Earned Income

Page 56: The percentage of expenses from the sale of tickets earned by orchestras is from the American Symphony Orchestra League. Information about specific orchestras comes from each directly.

Page 58: The percentage of the costs of operation that is covered by box office receipts by major opera companies was calculated by the Special Studies staff on the basis of information supplied by the individual companies.

Page 59: The Austrian Institute in New York City provided the percentage figure for the Staatsoper in Vienna. The figure for La Scala came from Henry Lee Munson, "Money for the Arts: The What, How and Why of Government Aid to the Arts in Seven Free Countries of Europe," H. L. Munson & Co., Inc., New York, 1962, p. 39.

Page 62: Information concerning lengths of season, size of theatre, price of tickets, and operating costs is based on an analysis of information received from individual theatres by the Special Studies staff.

Page 63: The percentage of income received by orchestras from broadcasting or recording is based on information received from the Boston, New York, and Philadelphia orchestras and from the American Symphony Orchestra League.

Chapter 4 Individual Giving to the Performing Arts

Page 67: The estimate of total contributions for the performing arts was calculated by the Special Studies staff on the basis of information from *Giving USA*, American Association of Fund-Raising Counsel, Inc., 1964 edition.

Page 68: Corporate income before taxes was $37.4 billion in 1958; in 1963 it was $51.3 billion. Source: U.S.

Department of Commerce, *Survey of Current Business*, July 1964, p. 8.

Page 72: Helen M. Thompson, executive vice president, American Symphony Orchestra League, made the estimate on percentage of contributions to orchestras. Figures for the Boston Symphony Orchestra were obtained directly.

Page 79: Figures on money raised by the Cincinnati United Fine Arts Fund, the Dallas Community Arts Fund, the Saint Paul Council of Arts and Sciences, and the Winston-Salem Arts Council were obtained from each council. Other councils that conduct fund-raising campaigns are the Allied Arts Council of Metropolitan Mobile, the Arts Council of Greater Fort Worth, the Cultural Attractions Fund for Greater New Orleans, the Fort Wayne Fine Arts Fund, the Greater St. Louis Arts Council, the Louisville Fund, the Memphis Arts Council, the Quincy Society of Fine Arts in Illinois, the Roberson Memorial Center in Binghamton, New York, and the United Arts Fund in Charlotte, North Carolina. General information about arts councils was obtained from Arts Councils of America.

Chapter 5 Corporate Support for the Performing Arts

Page 81: The factual information about corporate giving to the arts is from a paper prepared for this study and from a survey of corporations made by the Fund in the fall of 1963. Questionnaires were mailed to 135 corporations requesting information on each corporation's support and encouragement of performing arts groups. Seventy-three replies to the questionnaire were received and twenty-seven companies were contacted through personal interview.

Page 82: The corporate income tax rate was 52 percent in 1963, 50 percent in 1964, 48 percent in 1965. Percentages are from the Internal Revenue Code (section 11).

The Internal Revenue Code (section 170) permits

deduction for gifts to a "corporation, trust, or community chest, fund, or foundation . . . created or organized in the United States . . . [and] organized and operated exclusively for religious, charitable, scientific, literary, or educational purposes or for the prevention of cruelty to children or animals." Contributions over five years may be averaged in determining the tax-free 5 percent.

Page 82: Corporate income before taxes in 1964 was approximately $58 billion.

Page 83: Statistics on corporate giving for civic and cultural purposes are from *Report on Company Contributions for 1962,* reprinted from *Business Management Record,* National Industrial Conference Board, New York, 1963, pp. 24–33.

Page 83: Information on the percentage of total contributions directed by corporations to cultural activities is from *Corporate Contributions Report,* 3rd ed., American Society of Corporate Secretaries, Inc., New York, 1964, pp. 2, 10.

Page 84: Cost estimate of the amount to be spent on new construction of arts centers was obtained from Arnold Mitchell, *Marketing the Arts,* Stanford Research Institute, Menlo Park, California, 1962, pp. 5, 9, 15.

Page 86: Figures on corporate giving to education, health, and welfare were obtained from *Report on Company Contributions for 1962, op. cit.,* p. 25.

Page 89: The John M. Will quotation is taken from "The Admiral and the Opera," *Opera News,* December 7, 1963, p. 16.

Page 90: The quotation is from a letter from J. B. Perkins, president of the Hill Acme Company, Cleveland, Ohio, June 9, 1964.

Chapter 6 Foundation Support for the Performing Arts

Page 94: The information about foundation contributions to the arts is from a paper prepared for this study based on extensive interviews and correspondence with executives of philanthropic institutions and performing arts organizations.

Page 96: The description of foundations is from the Foundation Library Center, *The Foundation Directory,* 2nd ed., Russell Sage Foundation, New York, 1964, pp. 10, 18, 22.

Page 98: General figures and estimates on foundation giving were obtained from the Foundation Library Center. Information about specific foundations and arts organizations was obtained from each directly.

Chapter 7 Government and the Arts

Page 111: Unless indicated otherwise material concerning the performing arts in Europe in this chapter and throughout the report was derived from "Government Support to the Performing Arts in Western Europe," prepared for this study by John E. Booth of the Twentieth Century Fund. The paper surveys support in Austria, France, Germany, Great Britain, and Sweden.

Information concerning Canada is from an address by Dr. A. W. Trueman, director of the Canada Council, "Horizons of Progress," presented to the Roberson Memorial Center, Binghamton, New York, April 13, 1964.

Page 112: The Lincoln quotation is from "Fragment on Government," as quoted in *The American Treasury: 1455–1955,* edited by Clifton Fadiman, Harper & Brothers, New York, 1955, pp. 316–317.

Page 113: Illustrations concerning state and local government are derived largely from a paper prepared for this study. The background survey for the paper covered Arizona, California, Colorado, Michigan, New Hampshire, New York, North Carolina, and Washington; cities within these states and a few cities in other states.

Page 115: Governor McKeldin's statement was made to the panel on March 9, 1964.

Page 123: New York ranks fifth among the states in per capita personal income ($2,930) and North Carolina forty-third ($1,732) according to 1962 figures from the Department of Commerce, Office of Business Economics, as reported in *World Almanac,* 1964 edition, p. 748.

Page 124: States that have arts councils or commissions authorized by legislative sanction or executive order include California, Connecticut, Florida, Georgia, Hawaii, Illinois, Indiana, Louisiana, Massachusetts, Michigan, Minnesota, Missouri, Nebraska, Nevada, New Jersey, New York, North Carolina, Oklahoma, Rhode Island, Utah, Washington, and Wisconsin.

Page 128: A North Carolina State Arts Council was established in December 1964 by executive order. It is a temporary organization with no state funds. One of its duties is to develop recommendations relating to a permanent organization.

Page 129: Information concerning federal programs in the arts was obtained from papers prepared for this study, from Miss Barbara Donald, from correspondence with the departments of Defense, State, Commerce, and Health, Education, and Welfare, the Federal Communications Commission, the Urban Renewal Administration, and the Library of Congress.

Page 130: The Washington quotation is from a statement by Hubert H. Humphrey recorded in *Government and the Arts,* Hearings before a Special Subcommittee of the Committee on Labor and Public Welfare on S. 741, S. 785, and S. 1250, 87th Cong., 2nd Sess., August 1962, p. 263.

Page 130: Material concerning the Federal Theatre Project is from Hallie Flanagan, *Arena,* Duell, Sloan and Pearce, New York, 1940.

Page 139: In the Revenue Act of 1963 a charitable contribution deduction of an additional 10 percent (for a total of 30 percent) was allowed for certain organizations. In the Report of the Committee on Ways and Means, to accompany H.R. 8363, 88th Cong., 1st Sess., September 13, 1963, p. 53, it is stated that the many types of organizations that will now qualify for the total 30 percent deduction include "publicly or governmentally supported . . . community centers to promote the arts, organizations providing facilities for the support of an opera, symphony orchestra, ballet, or repertory drama. . . ."

Page 142: Information about annual revenues is from the Federal Communications Commission, *AM–FM Broadcast Financial Data—1963,* October 9, 1964; about dollar volume of the sales of stations is from *Broadcasting,* February 17, 1964, p. 100.

Page 143: The reference to taxes in Italy used to support the arts is from Frederick Dorian, *Commitment to Culture: Art Patronage in Europe, Its Significance for America,* University of Pittsburgh Press, Pittsburgh, Pennsylvania, 1964, p. 69.

Page 146: The study referred to on the professional performing arts in Europe is by John E. Booth, *op. cit.*

Chapter 8 Organization and Management of the Arts

Page 154: Study of Legal Documents of Symphony Orchestras, American Symphony Orchestra League, Vienna, Virginia, 1958.

Page 162: The principal craft unions are Actors' Equity Association, American Guild of Musical Artists (AGMA), American Federation of Musicians (AFM), International Alliance of Theatrical and Stage Employees (IATSE), United Scenic Artists, Association of Theatrical Press Agents and Managers (ATPAM), and a few others.

Page 166: The general description of arts councils is from a paper prepared for this study. Details concerning specific councils were obtained from each directly.

Page 169: The American National Theatre and Academy (ANTA) was incorporated by a congressional charter in 1935, but did not become active until after the war. ANTA, which has two theatres in New York, encourages theatrical productions of high caliber, promotes the idea of a national theatre, and attempts to stimulate public interest in theatre. ANTA has over 4,500 institutional and individual members. Its activities include theatre information and referral service, theatre organization advisory service, placement and job counseling, guest artist and speakers program, and photographic loan service. It publishes service pamphlets, news bulletins, and an annual report. Since 1959 ANTA has periodically held national assemblies.

The Central Opera Service (COS) was founded in 1954 under the sponsorship of the National Council of the Metropolitan Opera Association to foster a closer association among opera groups throughout the country and to encourage national interest in opera. COS has about five hundred members. Its services include information on repertory, availability of translations and musical materials, opportunities for obtaining scenery and costumes, public relations techniques, and management tools. A national conference is held biennially; regional conferences are held in the alternate years. Among its publications are news bulletins, and lists of opera groups, performances, and awards available to singers.

The Theatre Communications Group (TCG), established in 1961, is an autonomous nonprofit organization concerned with facilitating communication among nonprofit professional theatres in the United States in order to improve their artistic standards. TCG is financed by grants from the Ford Foundation. Originally offering its services only to member theatres, TCG now offers services to any nonprofit professional theatre seeking assistance. TCG's activities are divided into "projects," which include a visitation program, a casting information service, annual auditions for outstanding graduates of educational theatre, an observership program for directors and other personnel, and a consultant program for production and administration.

Chapter 9 The University and the Professional Performing Arts

Page 172: Background material about university activity in regard to the performing arts was presented to the panel in a staff paper. Specific details about universities were obtained from each directly.

Page 175: The National Council of the Arts in Education, organized in 1958, is a federation of national associations serving the various arts in education. Its purpose is to increase the articulation between the various art fields and the academic world. It has held annual conferences since 1962.

Chapter 10 Building Greater Appreciation

Page 188: The survey described was made in the spring of 1964 by the Special Studies staff with the cooperation of the Columbia Broadcasting System. Questionnaires were answered by 250 radio and television station managers across the country giving information on: live professional performances of theatre, opera, dance, or concert music in each station's area; increase in attendance at such performances; groups or individuals responsible for any increase in attendance; and the role of mass media in audience development.

Page 195: The Howard Taubman quotation is from *The New York Times,* June 30, 1964.

Papers Prepared for the Study

THE PERFORMING ARTS IN THE UNITED STATES

Music-Opera

Opera in the United States, by Richard Schickel; research by Mary Cronin. A survey of opera-producing companies in this country; problems and prospects.

Symphony Orchestras in America, by Joseph Roddy, senior editor, *Look;* research by Mia Fritsch Agee. A survey of symphony orchestras in America—physical facilities, schedules, income, budgets. Discusses their nonfinancial as well as financial problems and explores possible solutions for them.

Chamber Music in the United States, by Stephen Benedict, Rockefeller Brothers Fund, and Mordechai Sheinkman, composer. The present state of chamber music and future opportunities. Discusses typical problems of various groups; techniques and problems of management; foundation and government support for chamber music.

Choral Music in the United States, by Stephen Benedict, Rockefeller Brothers Fund, and Mordechai Sheinkman, composer. Considers professional and amateur choruses and choristers—their problems; suggestions for improvement.

Problems Confronting the American Composer, by Lester Trimble, professor of music, University of Maryland; former general manager, American Music Center. Economic plight of the composer, the performing musician, the concert-giving organization. How academic institutions, commercial organizations, and concert-giving organizations affect the composer. Recommendations and comments were obtained in a meeting attended by Milton Babbitt, Jack Beeson, Mordechai Sheinkman, Peter Westergaard, Yehudi Wyner, and Mr. Trimble.

Economics and Motivations of the Freelance Musician, by Melvin Ira Kaplan, oboist and entrepreneur. Economic realities of the freelance musician from the point of view of the producer as well as the musician and their effect on music-making in America.

Theatre

The American Theatre—Today and Tomorrow, by Norris Houghton, chairman, Department of Drama, Vassar; co-founder of the Phoenix Theatre. A discussion of problems of the American stage—the decline of Broadway and the growth of professional noncommercial theatre.

The Economic Problems of the American Theatre, by Murray Teigh Bloom, freelance writer; research by Mia Fritsch Agee. A survey of the organization and operations of Broadway and off-Broadway, touring and resident companies, amateur community and university theatres, and high school and children's theatres. Outlines their financial structure, sources of income; assesses major problems and proposes solutions. Includes lists of theatres and theatrical organizations across the country.

The Broadway Producer, by Stuart W. Little, theatre news reporter, *New York Herald Tribune.* Conditions and operating methods on Broadway today; "economic squeeze" on the producer and suggestions for ameliorating the economic climate of Broadway. Contains sketches of experiences of four individual producers.

Off-Broadway Theatre, by Richard Barr, producer. A look at off-Broadway: size of theatres, ticket prices, actors' salaries, costs, union arrangements, financing. Includes sample budget for a production.

Characteristics and Development of the Off-Broadway Theatre Movement, by Norris Houghton, chairman, Department of Drama, Vassar; co-founder of the Phoenix Theatre. History of the off-Broadway theatre movement; its economic problems and their relation to artistic fulfillment; institutional characteristics, development and support. This paper was partially based on discussions at a meeting attended by Julian Beck, Warren Enters, Judith Malina, Theodore Mann, and David Ross.

Problems of the Professional Playwright, by Irwin Karp, lawyer, Hays, St. John, Abramson & Heilbron. Among the problems considered specifically are copyright, "market places" for the playwright's work, the playwright's "investment," and the ordeal of first production.

The Amateur and the Professional in the American Theatre, by Dick Moore and Jack Golodner. Contrasts the philosophies, advocates, and aims of the two types of theatre. Bibliography.

Dance

Dance in America, by Richard Schickel; research by Mary Cronin. A survey of professional ballet and modern dance groups; their present dilemmas and possibilities for the future; existing foundation and government support. Also considers commercial dance, teaching, and the amateur movement for regional dance groups.

Economics of the Dance, by Richard Witkin, *The New York Times.* Brief survey of the economics of different types of dance companies in the country, financial problems of the individual dancer and choreographer, and some recommendations for improving existing conditions.

PRIVATE SUPPORT FOR THE ARTS

Foundation Support for the Performing Arts, by Marilyn L. Shapiro, Special Studies Project, Rockefeller Brothers Fund. How much of the philanthropic dollar goes to the performing arts, foundation reasoning for and against support for the performing arts, factors that encourage and discourage support, recommendations for improving relations between arts organizations and foundations.

Corporate Support of the Performing Arts, by Richard Eells, adjunct professor of business and executive editor of the Program of Studies of the Modern Corporation of the Graduate School of Business, Columbia University. Includes chapters on trends in American corporate support of cultural activities, corporate donative power, the business-culture nexus, educational dimensions of the performing arts, and freedom and the performing arts.

The University and the Performing Arts, by Alan L. Campbell, Special Studies Project, Rockefeller Brothers Fund. Performing arts programs conducted by universities —the advantages and problems of these programs and indicated lines of action.

Role of Labor in Support of the Performing Arts, by A. H. Raskin. How labor groups are trying to encourage greater participation in and support for performing arts activities. Also a section on what similar groups in Western Europe are doing.

Individual Support for the Arts, by Mia Fritsch Agee, Special Studies Project, Rockefeller Brothers Fund. A breakdown of where individual contributions come from, where they go, and how they are used.

GOVERNMENT AND THE ARTS

Federal Support for the Performing Arts: Programs and Prospects, by Robert Bendiner, author of *Obstacle Course on Capitol Hill.* Evaluation of existing government activities that involve the performing arts. The case against federal aid—with rebuttals. What the government might do to promote the performing arts.

The Federal Government and the Performing Arts, by Andrew Hacker, Department of Government, Cornell University. Brief history of government attitude toward the arts—from Puritan disdain to the Federal Theatre Project to recent congressional and presidential proposals to encourage the development of the arts. Considers the risks involved in federal support, the question of "quality" versus "equality," patronage and the artist, more beneficial forms government aid might take.

Taxes and the Performing Arts and *Copyright and the Performing Arts,* by Mia Fritsch Agee, Special Studies Project, Rockefeller Brothers Fund. Staff working papers dealing with taxes and copyright as they affect the individual artist and the arts organization and how revision would benefit both. Drawn largely from a series of meetings with Herman Finkelstein, general counsel for ASCAP; Irwin Karp, lawyer, Hays, St. John, Abramson & Heilbron; Robert H. Montgomery, Jr., of Paul, Weiss Rifkind, Wharton & Garrison; and Harriet F. Pilpel, member, New York Bar Association.

State and Local Government Support for the Performing Arts, by John H. MacFadyen, former executive director of the New York State Council on the Arts, and Alan L. Campbell, Special Studies Project, Rockefeller Brothers Fund. How state and local governments are supporting the arts through legislation, direct aid, and education; with recommendations for increasing their support. Key individuals in the arts in eight states and forty-one cities were interviewed by questionnaire or in person, as were twenty-four state colleges and universities.

Government Support to the Performing Arts in Western Europe, by John E. Booth, Twentieth Century Fund. Based largely on material gathered from personal interviews with producers, directors, performers, playwrights, critics, and government officials in West Germany, Austria, Great Britain, France, and Sweden, this paper gives a broad picture of how government support of the arts in these countries has operated, how it affects the individuals involved, and the question of freedom under government support.

GENERAL

Community Arts Councils—A New Dimension in American Culture, by Ralph Burgard, director of the Saint Paul Council of Arts and Sciences. Outlines the arts council movement in this country; the structure, functions, and financing of the councils, their strengths and weaknesses; how they might become more useful to the cause of the arts. Includes a case history of the Saint Paul Council, lists of community and state councils, size of budgets of various councils.

Labor as Performer and Practitioner in the Arts, by A. H. Raskin; research by Louis Calta. Union activity in theatre, music, opera, dance, motion pictures, and educational television.

Summary of Hearings on Economic Conditions in the Performing Arts—Dance, Theatre, Music-Opera, by Anne

F. McGrath and Maryann D. Ellsworth, former education analysts, Legislative Reference Service, Library of Congress. Derived from the 1961 and 1962 House Committee on Education and Labor hearings, the summary gives throughout page references to the original material. It describes the present situation, gives facts about training, employment, salaries, unions, and records the various recommendations made.

Dance Bibliography, by Genevieve Oswald, curator, Dance Collection of the New York Public Library. Over 150 annotated listings, including books and parts of books, articles, reports from dance organizations, and domestic and foreign government documents.

Music-Opera Bibliography, by Jean Bowen, Music Division of the New York Public Library. Over 130 annotated listings, including books and parts of books, articles, reports from music organizations, and domestic and foreign government documents.

Acknowledgments

PANEL PARTICIPANTS

Alvin Ailey, dancer and choreographer; artistic director, Alvin Ailey Dance Theatre.

Reginald Allen, special assistant to the president and the general manager, Metropolitan Opera Association.

F. Emerson Andrews, president, Foundation Library Center; editor, *The Foundation Directory*.

Samuel Barber, composer.

Richard Barr, producer.

William J. Baumol, professor, Princeton University; co-director, Twentieth Century Fund Study on the Performing Arts.

Stephen Benedict, Rockefeller Brothers Fund.

Isadora Bennett, publicist; director, Asia Society Performing Arts Program.

William Bowen, professor, Princeton University; co-director, Twentieth Century Fund Study on the Performing Arts.

Julius Bloom, executive director, Carnegie Hall Corporation; director of concerts and lectures, Rutgers University; president, Association of College and University Concert Managers.

John E. Booth, Twentieth Century Fund.

George M. Buckingham, executive secretary, Contributions Committee, Standard Oil Company of New Jersey.

Henry B. Cabot, president, Boston Symphony Orchestra.

Harold Clurman, director, producer, critic.

Dana S. Creel, director, Rockefeller Brothers Fund.

Alfred de Liagre, Jr., theatrical producer and director.

Thea Dispeker, artists representative.

Barbara Donald, former assistant to August Heckscher in his position as special consultant to the President on the arts.

Thomas Dunn, music director, Festival Orchestra of New York; conductor, Cantata Singers.

John S. Edwards, manager, Pittsburgh Symphony Orchestra.

Richard Eells, adjunct professor, Graduate School of Business, Columbia University.

Donald L. Engle, director, Martha Baird Rockefeller Fund for Music.

Jack Golodner, legislative representative, Actors' Equity Association.

Herbert Graf, stage director, Metropolitan Opera, 1936–61; author, *Opera for the People* and *Producing Opera for America.*

Harlow J. Heneman, management consultant; partner, Cresap, McCormick and Paget.

Carl A. Kersting, chairman of the board, Kersting, Brown & Co. Incorporated.

William Kolodney, auditorium consultant, Metropolitan Museum of Art; educational director, 92nd Street Young Men's and Young Women's Hebrew Association.

Edward F. Kook, president, Century Lighting, Inc.

John V. Lindsay, congressman, representative 17th District, New York City.

Isador Lubin, Twentieth Century Fund.

John Martin, former dance critic and dance editor, *The New York Times*.

Theodore R. McKeldin, mayor of Baltimore and former governor of Maryland.

Peter Mennin, composer; president, Juilliard School of Music.

Howard Mitchell, music director, National Symphony Orchestra.

Carol Morse, executive director, Young Audiences, Inc.

Thomas Pyle, chorister, choral manager.

Elmer Rice, playwright, director, author.

Julius Rudel, general director, New York City Opera Company.

Terry Sanford, governor of North Carolina.

Paula E. Silberstein, cultural resources specialist, Bureau of Audio-Visual Instruction, New York City Board of Education.

Norman Singer, professor; administrator, Hunter College Concert Bureau.

Isaac Stern, violinist; president, Carnegie Hall Corporation.

Paul Taylor, dancer and choreographer.

Gid Waldrop, dean, Juilliard School of Music.

OTHERS CONTRIBUTING TO THE STUDY

Donald Anderle

Sally Spratt Andrews

Theodora S. Axtell

Robert C. Bates

David Boroff

Squire N. Bozorth

Shirley P. Clurman

John Ehle

Thelma J. Elliott

Hyman Faine

Arthur Gelb

Ann Gibson

Eldredge Hiller

Robert Lekachman

John McNulty

Ben Tillman Moore

Hobe Morrison

Paul Myers

Gertrude Podolsky

Patricia B. Prescott

David Redstone

Saul Richman

Mark Schubart

Harvey Shapiro

Marilyn L. Shapiro

Margaret Sims

Karin Smith

Roger L. Stevens

Alvin Toffler

Robert Wall

John H. Watson, III

Permanent Professional Theatres

1964–65

The Actors Studio Theatre
New York, New York

The Actors Theatre of Louisville
Louisville, Kentucky

The Actor's Workshop
San Francisco, California

Alley Theatre
Houston, Texas

The American Place Theatre
New York, New York

The American Shakespeare Festival Theatre
Stratford, Connecticut

Arena Stage
Washington, D.C.

Barter Theatre
Abingdon, Virginia

*Candlelight Playhouse
Summit, Illinois

Center Stage
Baltimore, Maryland

Charles Playhouse
Boston, Massachusetts

*Circle Arts Theatre
San Carlos, California

Circle in the Square
New York, New York

The Cleveland Play House
Cleveland, Ohio

*Coconut Grove Playhouse
Miami, Florida

*Country Club Theatre
Prospect Heights, Illinois

**Dallas Theatre Center
Dallas, Texas

*Dorchester Music Hall
Dolton, Illinois

*Drury Lane Theatre
Evergreen Park, Illinois

Front Street Theatre
Memphis, Tennessee

Hartford Stage Company
Hartford, Connecticut

Hawaii Repertory Theatre
Honolulu, Hawaii

Lakewood Civic Theatre
Lakewood, Ohio

The Magnolia Theatre
Long Beach, California

McCarter Theatre
Princeton, New Jersey

*Meadowbrook Dinner
Theatre
Cedar Grove, New Jersey

*Melodyland Theatre
Anaheim, California

Milwaukee Repertory
Theatre
Milwaukee, Wisconsin

*Mineola Playhouse
Mineola, L.I., New York

*Morris Theatre
Morristown, New Jersey

Mummers Theatre
Oklahoma City,
Oklahoma

*Musicarnival
West Palm Beach, Florida

New York Shakespeare
Festival
New York, New York

Old Globe Theatre
San Diego, California

*Old Log Theatre
Excelsior, Minnesota

Paper Mill Playhouse
Millburn, New Jersey

Peterborough Players
Peterborough, New Hampshire

*Pheasant Run Playhouse
St. Charles, Illinois

Phoenix Theatre
New York, New York

**The Playhouse
Pittsburgh, Pennsylvania

Playhouse in the Park
Cincinnati, Ohio

*Playhouse-on-the-Mall
Paramus, New Jersey

Pocket Theatre
Atlanta, Georgia

Professional Theatre Program
Ann Arbor, Michigan

*Royal Poinciana Playhouse
Palm Beach, Florida

Seattle Repertory Theatre
Seattle, Washington

*Sombrero Playhouse
Phoenix, Arizona

*Stagelight Theatre
Wheeling, Illinois

*Star Theatre
Phoenix, Arizona

Repertory Theatre of Lincoln Center
New York, New York

*Theatre Company of Boston
Boston, Massachusetts

The Theatre Group
Los Angeles, California

The Theatre of the Living Arts
Philadelphia, Pennsylvania

Theatre Saint Paul
Saint Paul, Minnesota

Tyrone Guthrie Theatre
Minneapolis, Minnesota

* Commercial.

**Nonprofessional. These theatres have been included because they have continuity of management and professional direction.

Major and Metropolitan Orchestras *

1964–65

MAJOR ORCHESTRAS

Atlanta Symphony
Atlanta, Georgia

Baltimore Symphony
Baltimore, Maryland

Boston Symphony
Boston, Massachusetts

Buffalo Philharmonic
Buffalo, New York

Chicago Symphony
Chicago, Illinois

Cincinnati Symphony
Cincinnati, Ohio

* The American Symphony Orchestra League classification for orchestras has been: *major,* those orchestras with budgets of $250,000 and over; *metropolitan,* those orchestras with budgets between $100,000 and $250,000; and *community,* those with budgets less than $100,000. In 1967, the classification system will be changed. The minimum budget for orchestras classified as *major* will be raised to $500,000. Orchestras in the *metropolitan* category will be those with budgets between $100,000 and $500,000. During the present transitional period, some orchestras listed as *major* have budgets less than $500,000, while certain *metropolitan* orchestras have budgets over $250,000.

Cleveland Orchestra
Cleveland, Ohio

Dallas Symphony
Dallas, Texas

Denver Symphony
Denver, Colorado

Detroit Symphony
Detroit, Michigan

Houston Symphony
Houston, Texas

Indianapolis Symphony
Indianapolis, Indiana

Kansas City Philharmonic
Kansas City, Missouri

Los Angeles Philharmonic
Los Angeles, California

Minneapolis Symphony
Minneapolis, Minnesota

National Symphony
Washington, D.C.

New Orleans Philharmonic Symphony
New Orleans, Louisiana

New York Philharmonic
New York, New York

Philadelphia Orchestra
Philadelphia, Pennsylvania

Pittsburgh Symphony
Pittsburgh, Pennsylvania

Rochester Philharmonic
Rochester, New York

St. Louis Symphony
St. Louis, Missouri

San Antonio Symphony
San Antonio, Texas

San Francisco Symphony
San Francisco, California

Seattle Symphony
Seattle, Washington

METROPOLITAN ORCHESTRAS

American Symphony Orchestra
New York, New York

Birmingham Symphony
Birmingham, Alabama

Brooklyn Philharmonia
Brooklyn, New York

Columbus Symphony
Columbus, Ohio

Fort Wayne Philharmonic
Fort Wayne, Indiana

Florida Symphony
Orlando, Florida

Hartford Symphony
Hartford, Connecticut

Honolulu Symphony
Honolulu, Hawaii

Little Orchestra Society
New York, New York

Louisville Orchestra
Louisville, Kentucky

Milwaukee Symphony
Milwaukee, Wisconsin

Nashville Symphony
Nashville, Tennessee

New Haven Symphony
New Haven, Connecticut

New Jersey Symphony
Orange, New Jersey

Oakland Symphony
Oakland, California

Oklahoma City Symphony
Oklahoma City, Oklahoma

Omaha Symphony
Omaha, Nebraska

Phoenix Symphony
Orchestra
Phoenix, Arizona

Portland Symphony
Portland, Oregon

Rhode Island Philharmonic
Providence, Rhode Island

Richmond Symphony
Richmond, Virginia

Sacramento Symphony
Sacramento, California

San Diego Symphony
San Diego, California

Syracuse Symphony
Syracuse, New York

Toledo Orchestra
Toledo, Ohio

Tulsa Philharmonic
Tulsa, Oklahoma

University of Miami
Symphony
Coral Gables, Florida

Utah Symphony
Salt Lake City, Utah

Wichita Symphony
Wichita, Kansas

Index

C

P